THE NEW FREEDOM

By
ROB CUBBON
RobCubbon.com

The New Freedom
Rob Cubbon

Published by Rob Cubbon Ltd. *http://robcubbon.com*
© 2016 Rob Cubbon

ISBN-13: 978-1540461476

ISBN-10: 1540461475

Contents page

Introduction

I'm writing this in a cafe in Chiang Mai – a friendly, cheap, and beautiful place in northern Thailand. This is my fourth visit, and I've spent at least half of the last two years here.

I've also lived in other places: Bangkok, Koh Samui, Ho Chi Minh City, Phnom Penh, Cebu, Prague, Berlin, and London.

All this time I've been earning money, which is great.

But that's not what "the new freedom" means to me. I've also been meeting amazing people, learning languages, growing as a human being, and working on my business – which is a labor of love.

Happiness and quality of life are my priorities.

This book will unshackle you from needless expense, get you to move your life online, and provide you with actionable strategies to make a living with more meaningful work.

The new freedom can help all of us live a better life.

What is "the new freedom," you ask?

The new freedom is the result of changes within our views on traditional education, employment, accommodation, nationality, money, and relationships.

The new freedom gets people out of their old homes and into new communities. It builds international teams based on talent rather than geographical location. It is the freedom to work and travel during hours that suit you rather than sticking to the rigid nine-to-five routine. It creates a life on your terms through the new convenience and collaboration of the online world.

The new freedom can mean spending less and sharing more; working less and earning more; traveling more; and discovering that there's so much more to yourself and this world than you ever knew.

The new freedom can be accessed by everybody, no matter where they're from. This book can help those tied to a location by family, as well as footloose young people.

When I set out to write this book, I had a lot of people ask me how to do this as a single female traveler, with a partner, or with a family. To research this, I spoke with lots of amazing people about their lifestyles, and it was one of the best things to come from this project.

It doesn't matter if you're married with kids or single; old or young; entrepreneurial or employed. The online economy, the cloud, mobile computing, and the Internet are already allowing more freedom into your life. The purpose of this book is to help you gain yet more of the new freedom.

About me

My name's Rob Cubbon. I was once working on a string of dead-end freelance jobs. I started a website and serviced web and graphic design clients at home in my spare time.

As I began working more from home with my new clients, I did less commuting to offices working for other people. Commuting in London's underground trains to offices to do crappy jobs was something I truly hated.

As the design work kept coming in, I continued to update my website and YouTube channel with useful content about web and graphic design.

Amazingly, after only two years, I was able to give up the freelancing work completely and spend all my time growing my business from home.

Providing great content helped build trust with my website's followers. It also enabled me to collect email addresses from my website. So it was easy to start charging for content as I was delivering products and services my followers needed. I sold e-books and e-courses to my email list as well as on platforms such as Udemy and Amazon.

I now have a business with a number of income streams – design work for clients as well as passive income from e-book and video course sales and, on top of that, affiliate and advertising revenue.

It's a six-figure business now. I grew it from nothing – I received no investment.

So my business was providing design services to clients as well as selling digital products. I didn't have to be chained to a home office in cold, expensive London to run the business. I could run it from anywhere.

In 2014, I put everything on the cloud, packed my bags, and flew to Thailand.

And, if you'll forgive me, this would be a good moment to mention a few resources on my website. My business has thrived on connections, and it's always good to meet new people. So, please pop by my website, the imaginatively titled *RobCubbon. com*, and leave a comment.

I have six free video courses on my site. The courses are about creating websites, WordPress, email marketing, and earning a passive income. This is some of my best content, and it is especially aimed at people who want to work for themselves, earn more money online, and live the new freedom.

You can get these free courses here: *robcubbon.com/freecourses*

One of the reasons I created the blog and the mailing list, as well as why I'm writing this book, is because I want to help people. I want to show people that there is an alternative to the daily commute and boring work because I feel incredibly blessed that I was able to escape from it.

But people have their doubts.

Firstly, there's the money. We've all got to earn a living, and online business is especially unpredictable. Being short of cash isn't much fun.

Secondly, there's the social implications. Entrepreneurship, as well as location flexibility, is outside society's norms, and that can be trying at times, especially when dealing with bureaucracy.

And then there's the uncertainty. This life is fantastic but hair-raising at times, and it certainly isn't for everybody. But I've found numerous tools and techniques to ease the transition and keep motivated when times get tough.

I've been around a bit. I've spent 20 years in employment and 10 years running a business. In that time, I've met many people. I personally know many successful and happy entrepreneurs. I've interviewed over 30 especially for this book.

Join me and discover the new freedom so you can work less and earn more, so you can escape your expenses and experience the best life, and so you can unlock your potential and enjoy meaningful work.

Rob Cubbon

Chiang Mai, November 2016

First Steps to Freedom

Your movement towards the new freedom starts with a single thought. The thought becomes a belief, which becomes the realization of a dream.

Make your initial mindset shift a positive one. Don't make your purpose to improve your life materially. Better to make your purpose to improve life for yourself and others.

The new freedom isn't about making money. The new freedom is flipping a switch in your mind that makes you happy regardless of the money you have.

People build their dreams around a number. What if they never reach that number? And, if they do, what if they'll then want a bigger number?

We are all different. We have differing levels of freedom, change, or risk that we're comfortable with. And these change over time.

Regardless of your background and what sort of person you are, you are reading this book now, which means you have a feeling that you want a better life. It's my job to help you towards this.

The absurdity of traditional life

Success in the traditional life was "ownership" of a car, "ownership" of a home, and a six- or seven-figure salary. Success with the new freedom is doing work that you love and living a life you love.

People with a traditional job are drip fed by a constant income. They rely on it. Their expenditure expands or contracts to fit it. This is dumb.

They're not even guaranteed that salary. They could be sacked, made redundant, or get sick. Suddenly they're not getting paid – the drip feed is ripped from their arm.

On the expenses side, spending the disposable income every month (or, in most cases, more) is equally crazy. Are the products and services they buy each month essential for their happiness? No. The activity of buying for buying's sake is never satisfying. It just leaves them wanting more.

Adding to the absurdity of the situation, salaries are used to acquire the best or biggest home or car possible.

Most people borrow the money to "own" homes and other stuff that lock them into a life of monthly debt repayment. The monthly debt repayment can go up or down, and the salary could be taken away. It's hardly ownership.

The absurdity can be summed up with this Ellen Goodman quote, which is often shared on social media nowadays:

> *Normal is getting dressed in clothes that you buy for work and driving through traffic in a car that you are still paying*

for – in order to get to the job you need to pay for the clothes and the car, and the house you leave vacant all day so you can afford to live in it.

This isn't ownership. The "possessions" own people.

You have to work so hard to achieve the "good life" in the traditional economy. So much so, you're too busy and exhausted to enjoy the "good life," even if you reach those dizzying heights.

The good life in the new freedom is about valuing worldliness over familiarity, valuing experience over status, and valuing time over money.

The new freedom is not needing to spend the money you have.

Mind freedom

The new freedom can be accessed right now. The new freedom **can not** be accessed by striving towards a future goal. The new freedom is all around us.

You can find the new freedom by desiring happiness. You can find the new freedom by deciding to do more meaningful work. You can find the new freedom now by resolving to live a better life.

The new freedom starts with a mindset shift. If you've made this mindset shift, the rest of this book will help you build upon it.

The new freedom is surrender. The new freedom is complete acceptance of your situation as it is at the moment and being happy with it. Only then can you achieve more freedom.

The new freedom is not spending months or years developing a new app that will make you a million.

The new freedom is not wanting to recreate your current salary, benefits, and everything you have with corporate employment, except for the daily grind.

The new freedom is not bragging about your amazing life or making people jealous about how much you earn.

Those that have the new freedom can be rich in the financial sense of that term. Or they can make only modest amounts of money. But those that have the new freedom are as happy in their work as they are in their free time, and they sleep well. They live an abundant lifestyle, their kids are educated and well-rounded, they can afford healthcare when needed, and they can donate to worthy causes. They are rich, in every sense of the word.

Is it really money that you want, or is it happiness? Is it possessions you want, or freedom from your attachment to them?

Freedom of mind is an essential first step.

Your mind is free when your beliefs, desires, and actions are all harmonized.

I find that my mind is most free when I'm engaged in an activity I truly believe in. When I don't even have to think about what I'm doing. Maybe when I'm doing creative work or when I'm helping someone.

What would you do or have you done for free? This can be your new calling.

There are many tools and techniques that you can use to access the new freedom. But to gain more of the new freedom, you first need freedom of mind.

Cutting expenses with zero sacrifice

People wonder how I'm able to travel the world constantly for years. That's because they think it's impossible to do it whilst maintaining their current spending habits.

Do you have a mortgage or rent to pay, car payments, a Netflix subscription, a wardrobe of clothes to replenish every month, an expensive restaurant habit, a desire to buy the latest gadget?

There are two sides to financial freedom: earning more (from a variety of income streams) and spending less.

It sounds simple. That's because it is.

However, it can be difficult to change your habits. If you've purchased $50 worth of clothes every month for a few years, it's surprisingly difficult to stop. That doesn't mean you shouldn't try.

I'm old enough to remember spending $40 a month on music. When one of the earliest crowd-sharing platforms, Napster, burst onto the scene, I instantly saved $40 every month.

You can make such savings with zero sacrifice. Cut down your spending and focus on what's really important, and you'll live a good quality of life whilst cutting off the attachments that keep you comfortable.

Iva Ursano was a hairdresser in Sudbury in Ontario, Canada. Sudbury is 200 miles north of Toronto. It has long, cold, snowy winters where the temperature can go down to -50°C (-58° F).

After coming back from a three-week volunteering stint in Costa Rica in 2015, Iva had a sudden realization: she was working to pay for an apartment and a car that she needed for work. She ditched the apartment, rented a room, sold the car, and left work.

Iva is now a freelance writer living and volunteering in Guatemala. You can read an interview with Iva Ursano at the back of this book.

Christopher Lee, 30, from Singapore, is a location-independent entrepreneur and a short- and medium-term currency trader and helps others do the same through his site *PipMavens*.

He is currently in Chiang Mai in Thailand and reducing his expenditure to a minimum – swapping chain coffee shops with cheaper local ones, foregoing motorbike hire, and keeping his living expenses down as much as possible.

Despite his love for currency trading and his love for teaching it, he is planning to retire in two years. I wonder if he ever will. Not because I don't think he'll be able to. The people who can retire early never usually stop working because they love it so much. This tells you all you need to know about the importance of loving what you do.

Cutting down on unnecessary clutter in your home is especially useful. There may be books, clothes, and other items that you don't care for that can be given away or sold on eBay. There may be a TV subscription you can stop paying – successful entrepreneurs don't spend much time watching TV.

Getting rid of unnecessary expenditures frees your mind, which will make other freedoms easier to attain.

One of the most important lessons in business is to not

spend money unnecessarily. Never spend all your initial profits. You must save your initial profits. Online business is especially unpredictable. A business should always have money stashed away, but you should also invest some of your profits back into the business.

This is not sacrifice. It's a paradigm shift. It's a recognition of what's important and what isn't – a recognition of what you can affect and what you can't.

It helps you to have gratitude for the simple pleasures. So you'll live like a king without spending money and enjoy the abundance that surrounds you.

Mindset shift

Maybe this chapter is wasted on you. Maybe you're following your passions, but it hasn't happened for you yet. Maybe you've already made this paradigm shift, and you're looking for the next.

Maybe you're frustrated because, despite your best efforts, you're still not feeling the full effects of the new freedom.

I was frustrated as well. I spent years being chained to the expectations other people had for me.

Eventually, I realized what I needed to do.

My Story: *London, December 2011*

I hate crying. There's not only what caused crying in the first place, there's also the runny nose, the pain at the back of the throat, the heaviness across the stomach. I'm not a big fan of tears.

I was crying, standing in the hallway of our semi-detached three-bedroom suburban house, with backpacks weighing down on my shoulders, trying to say something to my wife.

My wife, who was also crying, held up our Jack Russell terrier, Lulu, to say goodbye. When Jack Russells look at you with those big eyes, they melt your heart at the best of times. I don't know what my wife was trying to achieve with the man, wife, Jack Russell group hug, but it certainly didn't stop us crying.

I couldn't say what I was trying to say, not that there was anything I could say. So I carried my belongings to the car, and tried not to think about my wife crying in the house with only the dog for company.

I tried not to think about her. I tried not to think about her parents. I tried not to think about my parents. I tried not to think about the plans we had to start a family and to live our lives together.

There's no point thinking about sad things. Only sometimes, things are so sad that it's hard not to.

There was no better place to put my thoughts and energies

than my business. I loved my business. I was creating websites for clients. Yes, I probably worked too hard… starting work in the morning and not finishing until midnight. That's probably not healthy. I did it, though.

I would say that I'd messed up, but something told me everything would be all right. I had something to look forward to. There was a big prize waiting for me.

I don't know at what point in our five-year marriage we knew it wasn't going to work. Was it the first day? Or was it the last?

I had been immersed in entrepreneurial blogs, books, and podcasts. One of my favorite business books was *The 4-Hour WorkWeek* by Tim Ferriss. One of my favorite blogs was Cody McKibben's *ThrillingHeroics*. One of my favorite podcasts was *TropicalMBA* with Ian Schoen and Dan Andrews.

I was aware of the location-independent entrepreneurs who married their creative businesses with cheap cost of living and travel. I don't know at what point I decided to leave England for Thailand, but I knew life would be better there for me. This would have been in the back of my mind towards the end of my marriage.

One thing's for sure. As soon as my wife and I had split, I knew I was going to Chiang Mai. I just didn't know when.

I knew I could make my business location independent and that freedom was waiting for me.

Freedom from Employment

Most of our self-esteem, identity, and happiness come from how we make a living. This can often lead to confusion and equating higher incomes with happiness. As I've said already, it's always better to occupy ourselves with something we love rather than to follow the money.

It's a constant struggle in my life to keep this in mind because, as an online entrepreneur, money often dictates the merits of a new product or venture.

We need to concentrate on the most important things and discard everything else. So rather than suffering now in order to secure enjoyment later, we must continually remind ourselves to **enjoy the work we are doing now**.

There are many rags-to-riches stories in entrepreneurial broadcasts. It's occasionally inspiring to read how some guy "crushed it" and is now making millions while on a yacht in the Bahamas. But real success is usually unspectacular, slow, and sustained. Success with the new freedom is no different. It's about consistently providing value, being honest, and enjoying what you do.

It sounds overly simplistic to say "do what you love." This is probably hard to take if you're trying as hard as you can to make ends meet. However, the freedoms of the online economy are available to all of us.

If you have no business or other way of making money, you can try to find freelance work in your spare time that aligns with your interests. Maybe you love creating things. You can get paid to write or design on one of the many third-party freelance websites.

> There are many websites where you can find all sorts of work to do, and you can find them on this book's resources page at *robcubbon.com/kindle8*.

If you are new to freelancing online, there will be teething issues. It takes a while to get used to the platforms, and the clients you work with won't be ideal. They are not my first choice of earning an income online, but for many they are a stepping stone.

Many office-based jobs can be done from home – if you can do your job at home, you can do it anywhere.

By working from home, you are already saving someone's money (if not your own): office premises in the center of town are unnecessary. Commuting to them wastes money, energy, and the world's resources. Millions of people are able to unshackle themselves from work but haven't even thought about it.

The new choice

There are many different ways you can add new freedoms to the way you earn a living.

Even if you're working a traditional nine-to-five and don't feel as though you can just hand in your notice, there is still a great deal you can do.

You can ask your company if you can work remotely. If you can do your job at home, you'll be free to work without the distractions of the workplace.

There is an article at LucidMeetings.com called "How to Make the Case to Your Boss to Work Remotely." You could pitch the idea to your boss for a trial period or maybe only for a few days a week. You could negotiate a pay cut in return. If you succeed, you'll gain some important entrepreneurial skills. And you'll get a taste for the new freedom that will never leave you.

You can do your job as a freelancer rather than as a full-time employee. This is what I did as a graphic designer, and it definitely put me onto the entrepreneurial path.

There are several benefits to being a freelancer over being an employee. A freelancer works for numerous companies and therefore can spot best and worst practices. A freelancer becomes more adaptable as they work for many different organizations. A freelancer learns the important entrepreneurial skill of dealing with the "feast and famine" of irregular money. The addictive drip feed of a salary teaches you nothing but financial bad habits.

You can make extra money while working in the evenings and weekends. There's no shame in making $5 a week at first. We've all been there.

But the best way is to provide some sort of service to clients online – writing, translation, design, consultation, etc. And whilst you're doing this, you can build up an online presence that will grow as the years pass.

These are three ways to initially leverage the new freedom. But there are many more.

Do this, and contribute to a new world where people spend time doing what they want and less time in a traffic jam wishing they were somewhere else.

The new location

Freedom from employment – permanent or temporary – means you are free to live wherever you want in the world. There are a variety of locations where you can live well and very, very cheaply – these are listed in this book.

There are hundreds of thousands of people all over the world who are, at this very second, earning income in a "strong" currency, such as the US dollar, and living in places like Southeast Asia and Latin America where US dollars can buy a higher standard of living than in countries like the US.

This doesn't just apply to highly skilled people from the west nor to people earning "strong" currency incomes. When Polish undergraduate Jimmy Naraine was studying in a UK university, he spent 80% of his time abroad. All his lectures were online, and he returned, sleeping on friend's couches, for group projects and exams. During his final year, he traveled to more than ten countries, saved money, and got a solid degree. Jimmy is now a location-independent coach and online course creator. You can read a fascinating interview with Jimmy Naraine at the back of this book.

London-based husband and wife team, Robert and Liz Lewis,

trained to teach English as a foreign language. In 2014, they
quit their jobs and swapped expensive London for cheaper Ho
Chi Minh City in Vietnam. The ability to teach meant that they
could generate a good income from working only a few hours
a week. In their spare time they were able to build a Fulfilment
by Amazon business. Teaching also added the security of work
permits, so there was no need for expensive and distracting
visa runs (crossing the border to renew a tourist visa). After six
months, their Amazon business had grown to such an extent that
they were able to quit teaching and continue traveling in Asia and
Europe while building their business.

When Todd Squiteri found it difficult to get a decent job in New
Jersey, despite having a Master's, he decided to leave the US. He
did freelance work on Microworkers and sold his possessions on
eBay to save up cash to buy him a ticket to Mexico where he got an
English teaching qualification in 2013. Since then, he has taught
while writing his own music and fiction in Korea and Thailand.

Many non-profit organizations also provide accommodations
and living expenses in various parts of the world in exchange for
labor. This can also provide a temporary period of unshackling
that can be used to develop other income streams.

Unshackling can be permanent, but it also can be temporary.
Many firms will grant sabbaticals. Many companies could
sanction a short period of remote working. You could just go on
holiday for two weeks and take your laptop. Be warned: the new
freedom is addicting, and you may never want to go back.

Shorter periods of unshackling and location independence can work as testing periods for your new life. The experience will teach you a great deal about remote working, cloud applications, and your ability to adapt to new working environments. It's a win for you (and a win for your employer, if you still have one).

The new sharing

A plethora of platforms have sprung up to encourage peer-to-peer earning (and spending) online.

In the last few years, sites and apps have sprung up to make it easy to earn online. The new sharing economy can help you store up cash so that you can buy a ticket to – or buy time in – a place where you can live on $500/month. You can work as a part-time taxi driver with Uber. You can rent out your apartment for days at a time with AirBnb. There are dozens of sites where you can get online work: copy-checking, copy-editing, graphic design, research, you name it.

You can invest your money, sell your skills, rent your car out, coach, look after pets, get paid to take online surveys, get paid for naming ideas, share your household tools and devices – if there's an activity or a secondhand product you can sell, you can get money from it online.

You can use the new sharing economy to gain freedom from employment, either temporarily or permanently. You can also use these sites to save money in order to gain freedom of location.

For 200 (yes, 200) extra ways to earn money in the sharing economy, read *Buy Buttons* by my friend Nick Loper.

Online business

I had design skills (although not very good ones) in 2005 when I first set up a website. I slowly learned web design and managed to get work from clients who'd contacted me through my website. It took two or three years before I had freedom from employment.

Other people need new skills – or to advance a small subset of their existing skills – in order to earn money outside their traditional workplace.

Avery Breyer was a healthcare professional in Toronto, Canada, who is now living and traveling with her husband and two kids in Asia and Europe, supporting herself with freelance writing and selling books. Writing was maybe less than 5% of her original career. She needed to learn or improve this skill in order to unshackle herself.

But it's not difficult. If you can write English moderately well, you can command hourly rates of $15-20 and above. If English isn't your first language, then translation can be as lucrative. Couple these earnings with savings in expenditure, and then living with more freedom is instantly achievable.

It's possible to unshackle even the most location-dependent offline careers to location-independent online ones.

Dr. Shannon Weeks is a doctor. You may think that doctors are all shackled to their offices or hospitals – not so. Dr. Weeks is a board-certified primary care physician, who earned his medical degree in Portland, Oregon. He is also a naturopath and is certified in applied kinesiology. He consults with patients in-person and online through Skype in whatever city he happens to be living in (recently in Chiang Mai, Thailand and Porto, Portugal).

Here are some businesses that are common amongst online entrepreneurs:

- **Selling digital products to a following**. Pros: future proof because of the following; Cons: takes a while to set up.

- **Selling digital products using affiliates**. Pros: low set-up costs; Cons: dependent on relationships with affiliates and requires continual launching.

- Selling physical products through Amazon (**Amazon FBA**). Pros: leverages the benefits of the Amazon platform; Cons: competitive, dependent on Amazon, needs capital.

- Selling physical products through a Shopify website (**Dropshipping**). Pros: low set-up costs; Cons: dependent upon paid traffic and search engine optimization (SEO).

- **Affiliate sites** (creating websites that recommend products and receive a commission if products are sold through clicks from the site): Pros: low set-up costs; Cons: dependent upon paid traffic and SEO (search engine optimization).

- Software as a Service (**SaaS** – selling software through a site): Pros: potential for regular monthly income and growth; Cons: high developing and marketing set up costs.

- **Consulting/freelancing**: Pros: Easy to get; Cons: Active income and therefore not scalable.

These are only a few income streams you can try, and the pros and cons can be argued.

Active vs. passive

The above list of businesses all operate on a passive income model, except for the last, which relies on an active income model. Consulting or freelancing for clients is is the easiest ways to make money online. But it is active income. This means you are swapping hours for dollars. The only way to increase income is to either work more hours or increase your rates.

Passive income, on the other hand, is scalable and less dependent on your time. An example of passive income is the sale of digital products. You create the product once and then sell it multiple times. The potential to earn money is greater.

Those of us who live and work online ultimately strive for passive income. But it's harder to achieve and takes more time to set up.

Making passive income your only goal when you're starting out is usually a mistake. It's a lot easier to earn a living as a freelancer than it is to make enough money consistently from product sales. But you can do both at the same time.

The ability to earn passive income depends sometimes on an online audience. A blogger with an email list of over 10,000 subscribers and a moderate social media following can earn good money from digital products.

As I've said, I made my first "entrepreneurial" money doing client work. At the same time, I created content online and developed a following. Central to this is a WordPress website and collecting the email addresses of interested parties.

So, start with active income, and prepare for passive income.

The alternative is to work for months and months whilst making no money in preparation for the launch of a passive income project that may or may not be successful.

The most common source of "failure" in achieving the new freedom is this: someone stressing for months on end over a product launch that fails to deliver. I put the word failure in quotes because those who do this will still have learned important lessons.

People rarely succeed with their first product. If you want to sell products, then ship the first one really quickly and create the capacity to ship the second product even quicker.

New freedom entrepreneurs that enjoy passive income often do so from a suite of products over a range of prices. That takes time. So it's essential that you have some way of making money that you can fall back on.

Building an audience

Living with the new online freedoms doesn't mean a steady paycheck. However, there is a lot you can do to assure long-term profits, and building an audience will do this.

Let's say you're earning income actively. You need to keep on finding clients that want your services, or the money dries up. Similarly, if you're selling on Amazon or making money from Facebook or Google ads, one change to these platforms' algorithm or terms of service, and your profits could be similarly decimated overnight.

If you have an online following or you collect customers'
contact details, you'll always have income. You can secure those
contact details by offering something valuable online for free and
getting email addresses of interested parties.

If you don't think you can offer anything valuable for free,
you're wrong. Share your experiences. You may not be the best in
the world at what you do. But you're unique. The honest sharing
of your personal struggles is the best way to build an audience.
It's also the easiest and cheapest way.

Gabby Wallace was an English teacher in Japan who started
videoing her lessons. She quickly grew a sizable YouTube
following, and made sure to point some of that audience back to
her website. Now she lives all over the world, selling her English
teaching products.

Building up a following by sharing content on YouTube,
Facebook, Pinterest, or wherever is great, but you've got to get
followers' email addresses in order to "own" them. And Gabby
did that.

If somebody is interested enough in you or your business that
they are willing to give you their email address, this is a big deal.
It means they like you, and a few thousand people like that will
make a huge difference.

Once you have these email addresses, ask them what they
want and build it, and they will buy.

The runway

The runway is the length of time you can survive without a job before you go broke. All the ideas on earning more and spending less in this book are designed to lengthen this period of time.

I asked Dan Andrews, co-host of the popular *TropicalMBA* podcast and co-founder of a private community for location-independent entrepreneurs called the Dynamite Circle, about his first steps to freedom. He replied: "fixing my budget and debts." You have to get your finances straight in order to determine your runway. He went on to say: "the first step to entrepreneurship is treating your personal finances like a business."

The runway, or "making the jump," may or may not be a useful analogy according to your situation.

Some people are unable to leave their home and need to save up considerable amounts before they can leave their job. Others will be able to sell everything and move to a cheaper part of the world while freelancing quite easily. Others will take the middle ground – rent their house out on Craigslist or AirBnb temporarily and try to live abroad before deciding to sell everything

Shayna Oliveira had been working full-time in New York City for about three years when she asked to work remotely from Brazil – her company agreed. Later, she asked to reduce her hours from full-time to quarter-time – and they agreed again. This freed up time for her to teach English online.

Shayna transformed her life to be less reliant on her salary. She then gave herself one year of "runway" and an investment of around $2000 to see if she could make the side business work.

That side business became *EspressoEnglish* where she sells English teaching e-books and video courses. She can run the business from anywhere in the world with an Internet connection. You can read an interview with Shayna at the end of this book.

Different people will have differing lengths of runway and amounts of risk they're comfortable with. Some people would like to bank on an "escape route back to normalcy," where they can go back to the life they lived if everything goes wrong with their new life. Some employers can guarantee a sabbatical from work for a few months. But, typically, there's no turning back.

The process of making the jump

Everyone can add new freedoms to their life no matter what their situation or background.

It's not just about a young man from the west with coding skills jumping on a plane to Chiang Mai – although that is part of it.

If you're seemingly "locked" into a job and paying off a mortgage with kids to support, you can profit from the new freedoms as much as a 20-something single person.

Which of the following freedoms can you add to your life?:

- Can you supplement your income by working a few hours online on a third-party freelance site, such as Upwork?
- Can you sell or rent unneeded possessions through peer-to-peer sharing sites?
- If you're working for a company, can you work remotely? Can you negotiate to cut your workweek by half or even by three quarters?

- Are there any areas of your life (banking, bill-paying, tax, etc.) that are still in the domain of paper and snail mail? Can you put them online?
- Do you have a home office? See if you can work from a cafe for a few hours every week if you've never done it before.

Even the smallest freedom is worthwhile. Earning a few extra dollars a week online could lead to a new business. Selling unneeded possessions could lead to extra headspace and a shift in priorities. Working remotely in a community could lead to new connections and friendships with others who are experiencing these new freedoms.

As Shayna Oliveira says: "Don't ask, '*Can* I do this?' That's a yes or no question – instead, ask '*How* can I do this?'"

The new money and the new happiness

There are a million and one ways to make money. The new freedom is about finding something that you love that allows you to make money and gives you the lifestyle you want.

The biggest barrier to finding this is ourselves. We are never satisfied with what we have.

I will return to personal development, self sabotage, and happiness in a later chapter, titled: "*Happiness and the New Freedoms.*"

From the Cubicle to the Cloud

The cloud, as if you didn't know, provides shared computer processing and data to users anywhere they are logged in. We now have cheap cloud services at our fingertips.

This is the first rule of location flexibility and maybe the first rule of our online life: ***work on the cloud.***

You have to put all your personal and financial documents on the cloud.

If any part of your life can be put online, it should be put online. Online communication and financial transactions are recorded so you can find out "what was said when" or "what was paid when" without having to rummage through reams of paper.

All your banking, transactions, and taxes should be online.

I use separate accounts for my business and personal affairs. Always having a record of every payment makes filing taxes a breeze.

My various online businesses are incorporated into my company, which has separate bank accounts, credit cards, and its own PayPal account. This means that I can download the relevant spreadsheets at the end of the year and give them to my accountant. It's a similar operation with my personal taxes.

This negates the need to have paper bills gathering dust and having to duplicate all this information for the tax authorities.

But old habits die hard: I once had a ledger for my invoices. It was like a large, pale blue exercise book from school. I would faithfully record – with a pen, in columns drawn with a ruler – the invoice number, date, amount, client, date paid, etc. Years ago, I put it on the cloud. I created a Google Sheet (the equivalent of an Excel spreadsheet) on Google Drive. However, I used the Drive doc concurrently with the book. I remember taking the large blue book with me on a trip to Brazil. I'd been recording my invoices in the blue book for so long I didn't feel I could leave it in London. Not even for three weeks.

Some people have all of their life on the cloud. Some people still have masses of documents stashed in cupboards. Some people are slowly moving from paper to paperless.

Some people still love paper and pens. There's nothing wrong with carrying a notebook around with you to take notes and scribble ideas on. A Kindle or the Kindle app on your phone or tablet means you don't need to carry heavy books around. Again, some people still like to hold a physical book in their hands when reading.

And it's perfectly OK to have a foot in both camps. But the more you move your life onto the cloud, the more freedom you'll get. There will be no need to fill out forms or keep documents. Your personal and business affairs will be sorted out in a flash online.

Cloud storage

I was a graphic designer who had a love affair with a huge 17-inch silver iMac. When I first considered location independence, I got a MacBook and quickly realized that I needed to harmonize my computers.

Maybe you have just one laptop to work on, in which case you'll be fine. However, for a long time my laptop and iMac didn't have the same files or applications, and I quickly realized the importance of the cloud.

Make sure that all your files are on a cloud-based service like Dropbox or Google Drive, both of which offer storage and backup of one terabyte for around $100 a year. There are many advantages:

- You can access your digital work from any computer in the world.
- You can easily share documents with anyone else you're working with.
- If you lose your laptop or accidentally delete something, all your information is backed-up.

Cloud living is essential to modern living.

Cloud-based applications

Google Drive applications work as well as the main Microsoft applications (Word, Powerpoint, and Excel), and they have built-in sharing capabilities so that you can see a document being edited by another user in real time.

Use the same browser login so that all your bookmarks and browsing history is saved.

Email should be accessed by the web as well. One of the advantages of webmail over a desktop client is that you can access your mail from anywhere. Gmail gives you added advantage of various Chrome extensions that I now can't do without such as *Send Later* (which sends a completed email a few days later if desired) and *Auto Text Expander* (which expands often typed text with keystrokes).

Another advantage of these services is that when you get a new laptop you don't have to laboriously copy files or settings. Just log into the cloud app, and you're good to go.

Location-independent entrepreneurs rely on a host of cloud-based applications – far too many to list here. But a few of the main ones are: Asana for project management; Trello for team collaboration; Slack for communication; Skype and Zoom for video conferencing; Whatsapp, Line, Facebook, etc., for chat; and Google Maps.

A slow ascent to the clouds

As I've said already, making these changes is part of a process, not something that is achieved all in one go.

Some changes you will want to make slowly. But other changes are impossible to take slowly, like the moment you leave your home country to travel the world. The new freedom requires more of these moves.

But just as your first move involved baby steps, so does your movement into a more flexible digital world.

My Story: *Floundering Steps*

For most of my professional life, I was working as a freelance graphic artworker in offices in London. These jobs were not my calling, and I didn't like the work.

I was one of the vast majority of people – someone who worked because they had to.

Starting to live

However, one of the benefits of freelancing was that I could go traveling, sometimes while teaching English as a foreign language, for weeks or months at a time. In the 90s, I spent time in Thailand, Portugal, Brazil, Cuba, and Mexico.

Inevitably, this could only be a short-term thing. The fun stopped as I always had to return to the UK.

Apart from occasional travel, I spent most of the 90s in a continual dope haze – every evening I'd come home from work, turn on the TV, and roll up a large marijuana joint. However, by 2003, I'd begun meditating. I was exercising more, reading more, and drinking less. I'd given up my 20 cigarettes a day habit, and with that, I'd stopped smoking marijuana.

These lifestyle changes meant an improvement in my memory and cognition as my brain's neural pathways re-aligned. Suddenly, I had a huge desire for knowledge.

I was now interested in everything: Buddhism, NLP, hypnosis, psychology, computing, the Internet, forums, Napster, searching and finding information.

Sitting in my apartment, searching for music and information, I realized I could be the one producing the information rather than consuming it.

I decided to give web design another stab. My brain had had a couple of years without dope, and I could now get my head around HTML tags, CSS, and web standards.

Slowly, I managed to put together a three-page portfolio website created in static HTML. This took weeks or months, but I was absurdly proud of myself when it was "finished."

I probably patted myself on the back and said, "Well done, Rob! You're not as stupid as you thought!" However, I was a little premature with my compliments. The three-page website was ugly. And, more importantly, it wasn't optimized for search engines, and therefore, nobody was going to find it.

I was talking to people at one of my freelance gigs about it. And I was incredibly lucky that someone there recommended *WordPress*.

Getting clients

I carried on going from freelance gig to freelance gig, and if anyone asked for my details, I had my *RobCubbon.com* portfolio site with an attached blog in WordPress.

However, questions remained in the back of my mind: What if I worked for clients directly? How do I get people to come to my site and give me work?

I had Adobe software on my Mac, which meant I could do the work I was doing at freelance gigs at home. And, by this time, broadband Internet meant that file transfer was no problem.

In the summer of 2006, a Google search turned up an article that advocated creating more content to attract traffic to a website. I had a light-bulb moment.

As the weeks and months passed, I wrote more, and more visitors came to the site. I made WordPress power my entire site, getting rid of the my first three web pages.

By the end of that year, three companies had contacted me through the website to see if I'd work with them. Suddenly, proper companies were asking me to work with them.

Whilst working crappy jobs for magazines, newspapers, and advertising agencies, I was a little cog in the big machine. I did what I was told.

Now, I was being asked to do more creative projects and complete them from beginning to end.

I was being asked to do projects that were completely different from what I was doing in my freelance gigs. I was learning to say, "Yes, I can do that" and then figuring out how.

I felt totally out of my depth sometimes. I must have made a few rookie errors, but somehow I made it through the first few years.

My design skills improved. I improved as a business person.

I learned how to deal with clients. What to tell them and what not to tell them. Why communicating through email was so important as it recorded every nuance of the project. When to use contracts. How much I could charge.

I absolutely loved this business that I had grown from a spare room in north London. I never thought I'd have been able to do that.

And selling design-related services was a totally location-independent business. But it was many years later that I realized the full benefits of location independence.

The Freedom and Flexibility of Location

The practice of working at a set time and place is out of date. Location independence isn't only about guys from the US nomading around Asia for an extended gap year. Almost anyone can use location independence to enhance their working and personal lives.

We are all walking around with little computers in our pockets that we use for scheduling, connecting, and communication. Put these devices to work for you and gain more of the new freedom.

Many large corporations sanction their employees to work from home at set times. Increasingly, professionals are arranging sabbaticals or periods away from their long-term careers to travel with their spouses and families.

These new developments are increasing our online skills and adaptability.

You can use the freedom of location to leverage new employment and business opportunities.

Mindset shift

Just as allowing the new freedom into your life starts with a mindset shift, location flexibility also starts with a similar change of perspective.

What do you do if your laptop or phone dies while you're away from home? What happens if you or a family member falls ill while you are away? What if you find yourself with no access to money whilst abroad? All these fears will fill your mind as you start to consider a new life. However, the new location-independent life is, in a sense, like the old location-dependent one: challenges occur, and you deal with them.

Nora Dunn sold her possessions in 2006 and supported herself with freelance writing. She still hasn't stopped traveling. When she and her partner suffered a near fatal accident in the Caribbean, she missed the support of an extended family and friends nearby, but this was offset by "a beautiful community of local people" who took care of her. You can read an interview with Nora Dunn at the end of this book.

Near fatal accidents aren't fun wherever they're experienced. Ultimately, people find ways to work through challenges and overcome them. Difficulties are, in essence, no different from the challenges you face at home.

So the mindset shift for freedom of location is to adapt to and benefit from your experiences – whatever they may bring.

Research

Whether you are planning to do some work in a cafe for a couple of hours or preparing for years of continuous working while traveling, you will start with a bit of research.

There are many books, blogs, and sites on location independence and remote working. Some have been listed here: *robcubbon.com/kindle8*.

However, most people will do some basic googling before lengthy periods of remote working.

Device security

Always password protect all your devices. That way, if anyone steals your possessions, they won't easily be able to steal your identity as well.

There is *HiddenApp* which will tell you where your Mac is (works with iPhones as well), which can lead to stolen devices being recovered. For Android users there's *Prey* and *Cerberus*.

On Android, you can backup all your phone contacts to Gmail, and third-party apps will allow you to backup all sorts of information from your phone. There is similar backup available on iCloud with iPhone.

Online security

I have already talked about the importance of constantly backing up your online data on the cloud so that you can access your work simply by logging into a cloud storage site.

But the transition of large amounts of data to the cloud can take time. So I also have a physical external drive (a WD Elements USB Passport). I have this partitioned into two drives. One backs up my work with Mac's TimeMachine, and the other contains disc images of software I use regularly so that if something stops working, I can reinstall.

Even if you are new to location independence, you will be familiar with the practice of using free wifi in a cafe. Any information as it moves across a wireless network is visible to anyone with the right tools.

Always use Virtual Private Network (VPN) software. A VPN lets you connect to a server somewhere else in the world and encrypts all of the information that passes between you and it. Good free options include *TunnelBear* and *Cyberghost*, which can also be upgraded to unrestricted paid services. There's also *Private Internet Access* (PIA) and *Witopia PersonalVPN Pro*. Look for a service that can be used with both laptops and mobile devices and that specifically says it works in China. VPNs have the added benefit of letting you surf areas of the web that may be restricted in certain countries.

Don't use the same, easy to remember password for everything. I use *LastPass*, which stores all your passwords on the cloud, which you can access through their leading encryption algorithm security system. LastPass and other password storage services provide the added benefit of enabling safe sharing of logins with remote staff, freelancers, and virtual assistants (VAs).

There is no finish line in security. No system of managing your data is 100% safe. But apply the basics I've mentioned here so that the people trying to steal your information will move onto an easier target.

The new collaboration

As you start to work from anywhere, you realize that you are free to hire from anywhere. Even more, you are free to Skype call, group chat, and even start a business with anyone anywhere in the world.

The new freedom means we can source from the world's freelance workers. Many online entrepreneurs run their businesses with teams of freelancers and regular employees, dispersed throughout the globe.

Different regions are known for different roles: the Philippines for virtual assistants; the Indian subcontinent for programmers; eastern Europe for programmers and designers.

However, collaboration is a skill that has to be learned. I had mixed results with my early attempts at outsourcing. Finding good freelancers to do tasks with technologies and software you don't understand is notoriously difficult at first – when you're on a budget, even more so.

Proceed with caution if you've never outsourced before. Sites like Fiverr, Upwork, and 99designs have great freelancers. But briefing and hiring for jobs can be a minefield to the uninitiated.

So start slowly, but keep going. After a while, you'll build up a network of freelancers and employees and, hopefully, back-up freelancers and employees that do jobs for you that will free up your time.

However, there is one type of collaboration that I wouldn't consider at first, and that is to partner with someone.

Business partnerships usually only work with people who are already successful. If you are just starting to make money in the new online economy, a partnership is rarely a good idea. You need to have control over the important parts of your business. A business partner could disappear or want to do something else.

However, meeting and collaborating with other entrepreneurs are essential activities when you're starting out.

The new freedom makes meeting other entrepreneurs so easy. You can do this through Meetup.com, Facebook groups, online forums, conferences, or special groups. Communication and collaboration is also easier in location-independent "hubs," such as Chiang Mai and Ho Chi Minh City, where virtually every foreigner you meet is an entrepreneur.

The freedom to work anywhere you want

The new freedom gives us the ability to live anywhere in the world while earning money.

There are old people, couples, families, single females, and people from supposedly undeveloped countries who have used the new freedom to emigrate from their home country to live in places that they prefer.

Older folks can retire early to another country; employees can take a sabbatical abroad; some blue collar or seasonal workers work six months of the year in a strong currency country to live six months of the year in a weak currency country.

The new freedom provides the ability to move our personal affairs online, cheap air travel, the ability to earn money online, the ability to make money from our houses, mechanisms for collaboration, and many other tools. All these new freedoms makes amazing travel opportunities possible.

Freedom of location isn't about recreating your home country environment in a foreign field. It's about adapting to new surroundings and thriving through the challenges.

When I tell people they can live abroad, they tend to raise objections, like money, visa, taxes, healthcare, and safety concerns. I will address these concerns, but they tend to be important in the minds of those who haven't made the leap but are unimportant in the minds of those who have.

The media, especially western and American media, peddles fear. If the media painted life as innocuous as it is, the media would cease to exist. As a result, many people see life overseas as dangerous, corrupt, unhealthy, and at times violent.

People have similar illogical fears about living a life outside of "normal" nine-to-five employment.

All these fears can be addressed logically head on, but ultimately, fear dissipates with action rather than logic.

An address at home

We've spoken already about the necessity to put all your financial affairs online so that there's no attachments to your home country, enabling you to enjoy all the benefits of the new freedom.

However, it's also important to have an address in your home country where you can receive mail. This is especially important for banks, credit card companies, the government, and, if you have one in your home country, company incorporation.

So, cajole a friendly relative, mom, dad, or sibling to provide this address for you. If you have set up everything online and have gone paperless as much as you can, little actual mail will be sent to your friendly relative's address.

Tickets

Deciding where you want to live and work will be dependent on many personal factors. I've included a chapter on many of the most popular and interesting digital nomad hubs later in the book.

Once you know the place, or places, where you want to base yourself for the next few months, many sites can help you find cheap tickets. Even if you're planning to spend a long time away, a return ticket is usually the same price as a single, so make sure the return date can be postponed.

Many websites specialize in cheap long-haul travel, which you can find on this book's resources page at *robcubbon. com/kindle8*.

Travel insurance

Many location-independent entrepreneurs don't bother with insurance. This is because, for example, if you need some sort of healthcare in parts of Asia and Latin America, it will be available at a fraction of the price of the same treatment in the US. Or if, for example, you had a catastrophic accident that damaged your laptop, you could quickly buy a new one in your host country.

However, if you are traveling with children or with a health condition, or even if you just want peace of mind, then there are several reputable insurance companies that you can look into.

Avery Breyer, whom we've already met, is a best-selling author and freelance writer from Canada who has been living with her husband and two children for over two years in Southeast Asia and recently moved to Mexico. You can read a full interview with Avery Breyer at the end of the book.

I asked her about health insurance: "Health can be easily taken care of as long as you don't skimp on health insurance. Also, before landing in a country, we research ahead of time where the top-notch hospitals are. And before, or right after, our arrival, we ask around for referrals to good local doctors that we can trust … We also mostly tend to stay in places with easy access to an international airport and modern medical care."

Avery's family uses IHI Bupa, which is "a pricier plan, but they have a reputation for paying out and they can't kick you off if you get something bad like cancer. They're forced to renew you every year. And because we went into this knowing we wanted to travel extremely long term, possibly for life, we didn't want to have our travel dreams ending."

If you are considering insurance, two other companies you could look into are Insure My Trip and World Nomads.

More information and links about insurance, you can
find them on this book's resources page at *robcubbon.
com/kindle8*.

Finding a place to live

To live in various cities for extended periods of time, you should
try to rent apartments or houses for as long as possible. The
longer you stay, the cheaper it will be.

The best accommodation is usually found with your feet on
the ground, trudging round until you find somewhere you like.
But there are alternatives to this.

Keep your eyes on the "digital nomad" Facebook group or the
"expat" forum for the city you're looking to rent in. Chiang Mai,
for example, has several Facebook groups specifically for renting
or buying accommodations.

You could, at a stretch, employ a local to find accommodation
for you before you arrive.

AirBnb and Couchsurfing can be great for temporary
accommodations until you find something longer term.
Couchsurfing has the added advantage of allowing you to meet
and make new friends in your new hometown.

Making money from your place

Of course, there are two sides to the accommodations question.
Not only can you save money by renting in a cheaper part of
the world, you can also save money by renting out any property
you may have in an expensive part of the world. This can be

maximized by Airbnb'ing a property. You can pay someone to clean the property and to be on-hand for the guests while you are away. You will make so much more than you would from traditional renting.

After leaving his stressful job as an arbitrage trader, Jasper Ribbers went from making $24,000 to $60,000 per year from his house in Amsterdam on Airbnb, which has been funding his travels since 2012.

Getting your hands on cash

Traveling teaches you about saving money on bank charges and exchange rates – handy entrepreneurial skills. Although ATMs are virtually everywhere, they're not the best places to get your cash. If you do, you may be paying the bank $5 for every $400 you withdraw – and at a terrible exchange rate to boot.

It's much better to use sites like TransferWise and CurrencyFair to transfer larger amounts of money at a time. The longer you stay in a host country, the more it makes sense to open a bank account there.

An alternative for Americans is the Schwab Bank High Yield Investor checking account. There's no minimum balance and no monthly fee, and the bank reimburses all ATM fees you incur abroad. There are no foreign transaction fees, either.

Tax and incorporation

International governments have yet to come to grips with location independence. Your tax and legal situation will be different according to the country you come from and the country your business (if you have one) is in. So, please consult an accountant or lawyer to find answers to your questions in this area.

Here is Andrew Henderson from *NomadCapitalist.com*, a site that helps people increase their personal freedom, improve their financial situations, and intelligently diversify their lives:

> *"Figuring out where to pay tax, when you have to pay tax, and how to do it has become increasingly challenging as governments are unaware of how to deal with the growing number of location-independent workers, and nomads are increasingly unaware of what is required of them to get out from the grip of taxation."*

It is, of course, important to follow the tax rules. If you are doing any sort of business, it's usually best to set up a company and separate your personal and business financial affairs.

I pay personal tax in the UK (where I'm from) despite not living there for most of the year. I also have a company that's registered in the UK and pay corporation tax there, even though most of my business is not in the UK.

You must pay your taxes. However, you are free to choose where. Many people who are permanently working and traveling incorporate (register companies) in countries with low corporation tax – Hong Kong, the Seychelles, Panama, etc.

Visas

The situation for legally living in different countries, again, will depend on the country you are from and the host country.

You can find specific information by asking in your destination country's embassy, a "digital nomad" Facebook group for that country, or any "expat" forums.

Location-independent entrepreneurs usually work in countries that have nothing to do with their businesses. So this work does not take from the local economy in a conventional way. It's also almost impossible to get self-employment work visas in many of the places that location-independent entrepreneurs favor. So many location-independent entrepreneurs are on tourist visas while "working" online. Like the tax situation, this is a legal grey area and is unlikely to be sorted out in a logical way by governments any time soon.

You can usually stretch a tourist visa for two or three months before you need to leave the country. You are then free to re-enter and stay for another two or three months. "Visa runs," as they are called, are either a distracting pain in the ass or a fantastic excuse for travel, depending on your perspective.

Doing regular visa runs for years on end can raise eyebrows at international borders and can cause problems. So, if you are thinking of staying longer term in a host country, it's advisable to seek out a different visa solution.

In Thailand, for example, the single entry tourist visa is two months, extendable to three at an immigration office. There are also multiple entry, year-long education, retirement, and business visas that require a little more effort. Neighboring Cambodia, on the other hand, supplies year-long visas for less effort.

An alternative to remote working is to gain conventional

employment in your host country. You could teach English as a foreign language, for example. If you're working in the local economy, you will need a working visa, and you should sort this out with your employer.

In many parts of the world learning yoga, a language, a martial art, painting, volunteering, or by attending a traditional university can be a great way to obtain a longer term visa and absorb more of the local culture.

Whatever the country, you should always research the visa situation before you travel. And when the visa gets stamped on arrival, put the expiry date of the visa in your calendar so you don't find yourself overstaying illegally by accident.

Dealing with different timezones

Freedom of location inevitably leads to timezone issues. No matter where I am, I always have *WorldTimeBuddy* open in a tab on my browser displaying the time in Bangkok, London, New York, and San Francisco.

Many location-independent entrepreneurs live in Asia and conduct most of their business on the opposite side of the world. This may lead to a few late nights or early starts. But, generally, most business people you're going to work with are familiar with the new freedom and flexibility of location.

I noticed this as soon as I started working from Thailand with my web and graphic design clients. When I received an email, I sometimes wasn't sure if the client was emailing from Europe or the US.

I didn't have a policy of telling or not telling my clients that I was working from Thailand rather than the UK. Some I told; some I didn't. The reaction of one client was "lucky you," and they continued to work with me.

I've "educated" my clients to contact me by email rather than by phone – this is a good idea for so many reasons.

I also always use the "royal we" with clients. So, for example, I say, "we'll do this for you tomorrow." This gives the client the subconscious feeling of dealing with a larger company, which might be dispersed through different timezones.

So, the one time I had an issue and I had to let a client down by half a day, I said: "our developer who is working on this lives in Bangladesh." That seemed to do the trick as well.

Just as I think it's none of the client's business whether I use freelancers to complete the job, it's none of their business where in the world I'm emailing them from.

Freedom of location is becoming more mainstream – many corporate employees work from home on Fridays. You may find that the client you secured in London or New York is actually emailing you from the next cafe in Bali.

Freedom and flexibility

As I've shown you, freedom is extremely easy if you're prepared to be flexible. But, what if you're a single female? What if you have a partner? What if you have kids?

It's the same. I'll show you in the next chapter.

The New Freedom for Females and Families

I know you might be thinking that all of this sounds great if you're a single guy, but it's impractical for those people who have families or partners or for women who are traveling alone. I've interviewed a large group of people who are doing just that – creating the new freedom for themselves and their loved ones. There's no reason why you can't, too.

As a single female traveler

I'm not a woman, so there's a limit to how much I can reassure the women reading this book about single female travel. All I can say is that the women I've met on the road seem to get along just fine.

Jodi Ettenberg quit her law job in 2008 for a break to go traveling. She has been traveling ever since, and her excellent food and travel blog, *LegalNomads*, now funds her lifestyle. She says on her site that although women are understandably the ones who ask her the most about safety, her tips apply to and should be followed by both genders. Many are common sense:

- Carry a rubber doorstop to wedge from the inside of your room at night.
- Carry a safety whistle (which also keeps monkeys at bay, apparently. There is a whistle attached on the front of the Osprey daypack and other backpacks.)

- Try to stay in a well-lit area of town in accommodations with a 24-hour front desk.
- Watch your drink and certainly don't get drunk, especially if you're alone.
- Err on the side of dressing conservatively.
- Be vague about your hostel/guesthouse. Sometimes a casual conversation will lead to a question about what hostel you are at or where you are headed next. It's wise to stay purposefully vague or have a (faux) backup hostel or guesthouse in mind for those situations.
- Be aware that eye contact in some countries can invite aggressive behavior.

You can read a full interview with Jodi Ettenberg at the end of the book.

Iva Ursano is a freelance writer living and volunteering in Guatemala. I asked her about solo traveling as a female:

"It's terrifying, it's so scary. Fear is the biggest challenge. But it's very empowering at the same time. You're going to come across some crazy shit sometimes, and you just do it.

I've got to go and live life. I've got to do something for me. For 53 years I did everything for everybody else, I made everybody happy. And I got no joy out of any of that... I'm 53, and if I want to do anything, I better start doing it now.

My parents are dead, I only have one son, I have sisters, I have nieces, nephews and cousins and all that. But I don't live my life for them. There's an emotional attachment, of course, they're my family. But I've got to do what I've got to do for me, not for them.

You leave your family behind. But technology makes it so easy to be in touch with anybody at anytime… so people say "oh, I can't leave my grandchildren." Yeah, you can! You'll see them on Skype. If you want to hug them, you go home once a year.

You have to cut the ties to all those attachments that keep you in your comfort zone. If you don't cut those ties, you're always going stay comfortable, and you're never going to live the life you're supposed to.

A lot of people read all these stories about 'dangerous' places and 'don't do this' and 'don't do that.' If you're going to read stuff like that, you're never going to go anywhere. Don't read those articles, use your common sense! Don't walk alone at night at two o'clock in the morning in a city you don't know.

I live in [Guatemala], a "third-world country" where there's drugs and gang wars. But there's none here where I live.

Female travelers should not get caught up in the horror stories and use your common sense, and you're gonna be fine."

Natalie Jay, originally from Russia, left a promising legal career in 2012 to launch a B2B commodities import/export business. She told me that after four years of solo travel, she's pretty much had zero problems that she could put down to gender.

Princess Villareal is from the Philippines and has to carry numerous samples of the products that she sells. The major challenge she faces is with luggage: "Men can just bring a light backpack, and that's it. We women bring a lot of things with us. I brought about 50-60 kg of luggage from the Philippines to Vegas, to Chiang Mai, and to the Philippines again. It wasn't fun, because normally I have to take about three or four connecting flights, and the extra luggage fees are expensive." You can read an interview with Princess Villareal at the end of the book.

Dan O'Donnell, a former realtor from America, now makes money from personal development products on his Facebook page, which has a million "likes," and a board game called *Better Me*. He has been based in Chiang Mai since 2014. He started the Chiang Mai Digital Nomad Facebook group (currently over 13,000 members) and regularly meets with newly arrived entrepreneurs. When I asked him about lone female entrepreneurs, he recommended that women look for women-only groups and clubs in the regions they're traveling to, via Facebook, Meetup.com, or other online connection sites. Women travelers have formed extensive, supportive networks that help them navigate those issues that are most relevant and concerning to them.

Remember, the new freedom is accessible to everybody. There are entrepreneurial support groups for women in every major city and every major entrepreneurial hub. Chiang Mai is just the tip of the iceberg of what's out there.

Women's Entrepreneurial Network – Chiang Mai

www.facebook.com/groups/WomensEntrepreneurialGroupCM

Family and the new freedom

Family seems like the ultimate reason to stay shackled to a certain location.

In 2014 Paul Kortman and his wife, Becky, packed up their four children, sold everything, and began a life of location independence supported by Paul's digital marketing agency. Their kids are homeschooled in the standard curriculums, yet enriched with much more in terms of world exposure. Many similar stories are told on their site at *HomeAlongTheWay*.

Dan Cumberland of TheMeaningMovement began helping high school students find their purpose academically and professionally in 2005. Later, he built a counseling community inside of his graduate school. In 2011 he began working with clients professionally one on one. However, Dan suddenly realized he was unfulfilled doing as he was "supposed to do." Dan is now a writer, speaker, and coach, as well as a photographer at Sparkfly Photography, a company he runs with his wife, Stacia. Dan and Stacia now use their new freedom to work more at home. They have twice-a-week strategy meetings that are incredibly helpful to keep priorities straight and the business moving in the right direction.

Jacob Hiller created the *Jump Manual* ten years ago and has since sold over $6 million worth of e-books and created many other businesses. Soon after getting married 10 years ago, his wife got a job in Germany, so they left the US. They still haven't returned. At the time of writing, they have visited 65 countries. Four years ago, they had a son, who has visited 35 of those 65. He has been to school in Holland, Peru, South Africa, and Germany.

We usually stay three months or more in every country. I don't like to travel too fast because I like to kind of soak it in. I don't travel to see things. I travel to experience things.

We decided to have a baby, so we moved to Mexico because Mexico gives citizenship to the baby when they're born. (Brazil would actually give us [the parents'] citizenship...) So we stayed there for eight months to have my son, Ryder...

What's cool is every country has their expectations of what you should do with the baby or what you should not do with the baby. And what I love about traveling with a baby is that they don't have any expectations of where they're gonna sleep, what their next toy is, which thing you're gonna do... so Ryder, I feel, is extremely flexible.

He knows how to go through customs lines, he knows how to sit on a bus for 20 hours, he knows how to be on a subway, he knows how to do all those things. And he's just so easy to be around.

People think it's hard. But Ryder was born on the road.

He's lived in 35 countries, made friends all over the world, Skypes with his friends, and keeps in touch with family that way. Because we don't have family around, we made a great effort to make sure he's connecting with family on a regular basis. And sometimes he'll get on Skype himself, dial it up, and talk to grandma or his uncles.

We'll try to make sure we know where the hospital is but we've never had any problems.

We're in Germany right now, and Ryder has just started in a German school. He doesn't speak German. But he's really good at making friends and playing with friends even if he doesn't understand the language. Now when he plays with dinosaurs, he asks the dinosaurs what languages they speak.

For me, with the kid, everything is just more fun. You go to see something ... and the fact that he's there and he's in awe of it, just makes it that much more fun. Because we've been to 30-40 countries and things are still exciting to see, but you get to watch this little human being react to it and see it for the first time, and you share in that excitement.

Sleeping. A lot of times, Ryder would just sleep with us. He did a lot more when he was younger. He's very easy with sleeping. He can sleep anywhere.

Because he has always been on the road, he has always adapted to things and never has any expectations. It's just been a very easy-going experience for us.

We find babysitters locally. I think we wanna get an au pair next to make things that much more flexible. So we can go out anytime or doing anything we want at whatever time.

> *He's got his friends that he Skypes with, so now my next step is to make sure we can go back to those places. So he can realize when we leave a place, he's not leaving a friend, he is just leaving that country, and he can go see them another time. He's not saying goodbye forever.*

You can read a full interview with Jacob Hiller at the end of this book.

Worldschooling and the new freedom

As traditional school and university educations are increasingly anachronistic and unfit for purpose in the online age, homeschooling is on the rise.

The arguments against homeschooling (also referred to as unschooling and, the location-independent version, worldschooling) are that the child would "miss out" on both the qualifications and socializations of traditional school. Neither of these arguments are sound, according to homeschooling parents and children.

It's very easy to follow certain countries' curricula if required. Exams can still be taken by homeschooled children, and they can be accepted by traditional universities.

As far as socialization is concerned, homeschooled children have the privilege of meeting and getting to know children and adults of all ages and cultures through their parents as well as through online communities of homeschoolers. They also don't have to put up with the bullying or the trauma of needing to "fit in" at school.

Indeed, studies investigating how children naturally learn repeatedly find that they do so most deeply and with the greatest enthusiasm in conditions that are almost opposite to those of school.

There are downsides to home education. Some children can react against being uprooted at certain ages from a traditional school environment to a homeschooling one.

Avery Breyer has been living as a location-independent entrepreneur with her family (husband and two sons aged seven and nine) for over two years. I spoke to Avery about her experiences as a traveler, entrepreneur, and mother. Avery is the sort of person who wouldn't leave any stone unturned and proved (to me at least) that if you want to do something badly enough, there's always a way to do it.

I asked her about homeschooling: "The actual schooling part isn't hard – there are lots of online resources for homeschoolers these days. [*See below.*] ... The hard part is maintaining the patience to be your child's teacher and parent 24/7. You don't get a break from it for five days of the week like you do if your child is in traditional school. The patience thing is a work in progress, and you're always trying to better yourself, improve your ability to be understanding through all of your child's ups and downs."

For math, Avery's kids use an app called *Dreambox* on their iPads, which follows the US curriculum and Ontario, Canadian curriculum. For reading, they use *Hooked on Phonics*. And

ReadingPro is available from the same company for older kids.

Avery was in Mexico when I spoke to her and had just gotten back from a worldschooler's meetup. Thanks to social media, Avery's family can instantly connect with other families who are traveling and worldschooling anywhere in the world. They can compare notes with other parents, and their kids can meet other kids with similar experiences. The Internet is opening up new connections, both local and global, for families (as well as individuals) to gain more of the new freedom.

James Allen was living and teaching English in Japan in 2003 when his wife became pregnant with their only daughter. He was determined to use the technology that was freeing up traditional concepts of work and living to also free his new child from the constraints and failures of traditional education.

After searching products in Japan that could be sold online for a profit, he stumbled across a product that was cheap to source in Japan and could be sold at a markup on eBay. By the time his daughter was born in early 2004, he was making a full-time living selling and exporting underground comic books and was able to quit his teaching position just in time for her birth.

Since she was born and raised in Japan, they followed some Japanese curricula for reading, writing, and math.

James was responsible for her English in the home while her mother was responsible for keeping her on track with Japanese studies.

The family has been location independent and traveling since 2011, and James's daughter has learned how to study in a variety of countries. Since then, she has had one year of traditional schooling in New Zealand. Workbooks were sent by mail from Japan to wherever they were and corrected by a private teacher.

As his daughter has gotten older, she's become more independent with her studies. For example, when in Bali she did intensive study of traditional Balinese dancing and was invited to perform at temple ceremonies. She speaks and writes Japanese and English fluently, can speak Indonesian, and has started learning Chinese as well.

Much of the process has been thanks to James's wife, who has spent the most time working with her on her studies.

James and his wife both recognize that a lot of the world still operates on the "old" system and that she might need to "prove" what she has learned through traditional examination. However, since she has been brought up in a nomadic, entrepreneurial family, she already has many ideas about how to do the same on her own, and she's already getting mentoring on her own online income streams like those she has been raised on.

Her current favorite sites and tools:

- *Khan Academy* for math and online math games at *Multiplication.com*.
- *Scratch* and *Code Academy* to learn Python and JavaScript.
- She has a Rasberry Pi computer that travels with her and uses courses on Youtube to study programming with it. She is currently working with Minecraft Pi to further study programming.

- She also spends a lot of time on YouTube watching videos on any topics that interest her at the time.

You can read a full interview with James Allen at the end of the book.

Worldschoolers Facebook group: *www.facebook.com/groups/worldschoolers/*

Travel is the new security

The people who travel never regret it.

Despite the fear-mongering in the western media, I haven't heard many bad stories from long-term travelers. Long-term travelers are usually more savvy and therefore are less at risk than short-term travelers and tourists.

We thrive in challenging situations that force us out of our comfort zone, and that is why traveling is good for the soul.

I recognized this during my first short periods abroad in the 90s. Too bad they didn't last longer. And too bad I had to wait so long to go away again …

My Story: *Losing in Love and Life*

When I met the lady who was to become my ex-wife – I'll admit it – I said to myself, "Damn, she's nice!"

I'll never forget a friend of mine at our wedding drunkenly saying, "I can't believe you've married such a hot chick!"

I laughed. He was only saying what everyone else was thinking. I was the guy that could never get a girlfriend, and then all of a sudden I was marrying someone who wouldn't look out of place on the cover of *Vogue*.

It took five years to admit to what we'd probably known in our heart of hearts on our wedding day.

But this wasn't really the end of the world, I had to keep telling myself. We never had kids. But we had a dog.

From the beginning of 2012, my wife (she didn't become my ex-wife for another two years) was living alone with the dog. I was living in a friend's apartment. I spent much of those two years traveling (or commuting) to our home to check on things. We had to decide what we were going to do.

The next couple of years were rough for us. But we got through it.

Divorce

I had two sets of well-educated lawyers screwing me for every penny at every turn of the long drawn-out process of divorce. Or maybe the lawyers were so bad they served to take my mind off what I was experiencing.

My wife's lawyer had received a post-graduate education in Oxford or Cambridge (he'd proudly put MA (Oxon) or MA (Cantab) after his name on his website, I can't remember which). A seriously clever dude. Not everyone can get into those universities, and not anyone can finish a Master's.

He must have worked very hard and have been seriously gifted. I remember thinking, why? Why work so hard and get a great degree at an internationally recognized university to shuffle papers around in a High Street law firm and try to screw homebuyers and divorcees out of a few hundred quid? Is that what his world was all about?

I thanked (and still thank to this day) my outrageous good fortune of discovering entrepreneurship.

Also, I had no friends left in London.

This was a shock. Especially when I thought back to those years when my phone would be ringing all the time with friends asking me out. I had a group of friends I'd play football with and other circles of friends I could call on when I wanted to go somewhere.

I'd been living in London on and off since 1986, and it was now 2012 ... Over 25 years of living in London, and I didn't know a soul.

The reason for this was financial. In my teens, twenties, and early thirties, my friends and I were renting apartments in London – sometimes sharing apartments with three of us crammed into a one-bedroom flat.

However, one by one, friends had had enough of the cost of London. They either returned to where they came from (sometimes to live with their parents) or went off to somewhere else in the UK.

And, of course, a lot of them were marrying and having kids and therefore wanted to move out of London to find a more affordable and maybe quieter place to bring up children.

So there I was in London, getting divorced with no friends for company. I immersed myself in my business and Meetup.com. The two subjects of meetups I would go to were entrepreneurial and spiritual. I met a lot of people whom I'm still in touch with.

I agreed on a settlement with my wife, and we never argued about it. (Quite an achievement when you consider we'd been arguing constantly for years).

With the money left over from the three-bedroom house, I was able to buy a one-bedroom apartment that I could rent out, pay a mortgage on, and get a little bit more passive income every month.

I tried to care less and less about money. If you lose a great deal of money, as I have done, it makes you realize how little you actually need it. I used to say to myself, what if I died tomorrow? I wouldn't be bothered about losing the money then. Now if I think about dying tomorrow, I'd be disappointed because I've only being traveling for two years, and I haven't enjoyed life enough (although I'm working on it!)

My identity as a husband had gone. My identity as a fun-loving freelancer in London had gone. My identity as as a nine-to-five'er was long gone.

My identity as an entrepreneur was all I had.

Throughout the long, dark months of my divorce and the feeling of losing money I thought of as my own, I always had Thailand as the beautiful light at the end of the tunnel.

Happiness and the New Freedoms

The new freedom will initially make you happier – the freedom to work for yourself and not for a "boss"; the freedom to work when you want; the freedom to travel and see the world.

That can make you happy for a few months, a few years even, but you'll soon get used to it. And what then?

If you work for yourself and don't have the routine of a nine-to-five, you have to have self-motivation to make sure everything gets done. If you're traveling a lot, you may have loneliness and culture shock to deal with on top of that. Plus, your income can go up as well as down. What do you do to cope with the "down" times?

Some of us were told what to do in school and at work. Suddenly experiencing the new freedoms of flexible living and location independence can leave us feeling disoriented. But there are many ways we can deal with this.

As I've said before, it's easy to confuse happiness with money. Happiness is ethereal and intangible – and certainly can't be quantified with a number.

Establishing a beautiful purpose

The most useful way I have found to combat entrepreneurial loneliness and lack of direction with the new freedom is, quite simply, to not take myself too seriously.

After working alongside Mark Joyner (the first person to sell an e-book), Leon Jay went on to work on several six- and seven-figure product launches. I met Leon in Chiang Mai where he'd lived for seven years building a team around his successful online services business. He told me:

> *"Sadly, I have found few who have found genuine happiness and life purpose through [the independent lifestyle]. Sure, many find it exciting and different at first, but without a greater reason than personal and financial freedom, most I have met eventually feel just as empty or lost as they did before leaving their desks.*
>
> *"Case in point, I was just talking to one of my friends who is now making more money in his life than ever before, flying business class, and about to sell his FBA (Fulfilment by Amazon) business for millions. He has never felt more empty and depressed and expressed this was due to what he was doing to make a living."*

Whenever I do something just for the money, I always get bored. I give up and move onto the next thing.

Going into online business to make loads of cash is dumb. Period.

Helping people

Having a purpose in your business and work that is 100% for the benefit of other people is central to your happiness with the new freedoms.

A cast iron determination to make lots of money will not

ultimately make you happy. It may make you bored ... and boring. Money, at the end of the day, is just a number. Assuming you have freedom from employment and you're building a business that enables you to eat and afford to live somewhere, more money will not make you more happy.

I try to cultivate a feeling of gratitude when revenues are down. I feel incredibly grateful that I still have this amazing lifestyle, even though I'm making substantially less this month than I have done before. I still don't have a boss. I still don't work nine-to-five. I still do what I want. I can still feed myself and have a roof over my head. I'm making less money than before. So what?

You're never as bad as you think; you're never as good as you think. You're you. And that's good enough.

Even if you're providing design, development, or writing services, you're helping people through your business. Later on you can consult for people and help them to experience more of the new freedoms. Helping people to become free and happy is a great purpose for a business.

You can establish gifting from your business right from the beginning. Start by giving $100 every month (set up a regular payment to a charity you like on PayPal – they will be grateful). Would you notice $100 missing every month? Probably not. Even if you're not making much money now, it's a great thing to do. And later on you can gift $500 a month, and then more as your business grows.

Helping people and working towards a positive purpose with your business will ultimately save you from burn out.

Even if your business isn't 100% for the betterment of the human race, you can incorporate elements of altruism into it. You can make sure you donate a percentage of the profits to helping people, as I've said. You can spend time on voluntary projects to support a less fortunate community. You could voluntarily mentor others. You could even learn new skills, such as cooking, language, art, etc. If you fall in love with something somewhere, learning about it will improve your quality of life.

The alternative is striving to increase the profit line every month, and everyone who does that eventually crashes and burns. There will always be bigger numbers to chase.

Slow travel

A "digital nomad" is someone who works online and lives in various places around the world that take his (usually a male) fancy from moment to moment. I'm avoiding this term both in describing this book and describing myself. Young men from the west may enjoy this lifestyle for a few years, but it's not sustainable in the long term.

Having said that, location independence has been hugely beneficial for me. I have more friends in Chiang Mai, a city that I've lived in for 12 out of the last 24 months, than I do in London, a city I lived in for over 25 years.

When you are living outside your own culture, your senses are bombarded with new experiences, which promotes an open-mindedness. This openness is picked up by others, and you make new friends easily.

However, there are downsides. As Nora Dunn says: "There is a whole contingent of location-independent travelers who have started to burn out (of which I'd say I've recently teetered on the edge)." After the initial excitement and adrenalin of traveling wears off, people can feel lonely and isolated. There are many ways to stop this happening, or make sure it doesn't happen in the first place.

Nora Dunn herself dealt with her issues while traveling in much the same way as she would have done at home.

If something bad happens to you, it's happening for a reason, and that reason is so that you can learn something about yourself. This is the same on the road as it is in your home country.

One possible answer to the traveling blues: choose one location as a "base" for your life and business and then take holidays!

A "base" gives you a network of friends and familiarity that can be welcome after a lot of traveling. I have gravitated towards Chiang Mai in northern Thailand for this purpose. I know people here, I have my favorite restaurants and cafes, and I'm learning the language. All this would be impossible with a truly nomadic existence.

So, if you're location independent, don't let it go to your head. Traveling is tiring and time consuming. Travel slowly, and find a nice place to base yourself.

Meeting people

Wherever you are in the world, it's always good to meet people. If you are trying to build a business, meeting other business people is especially beneficial. And it is usually pretty easy to do, depending on the size of town or city you are in.

Try Facebook. Search for the name of the city you are in plus the words "digital nomads." And then you'll find the "Bangkok digital nomads" or the "Chiang Mai digital nomads." There you will find excellent information on local co-working spaces, meetups, accommodation, and even work.

I have found *Meetup.com* excellent for finding events or meetups with likeminded people. Conferences are meetups on steroids and can be great for making connections. The *Dynamite Circle* is a private community for location-independent entrepreneurs that organizes meetups, conferences, and masterminds. If you join *NomadList.com*, you can connect with thousands of location-independent types and arrange meetups. There are also other nomad-type forums.

When you meet others, avoid trying to impress people. Entrepreneurs like to put their best foot forward. Of course, we all have to put on a brave face. And you'll always meet entrepreneurs who are doing very well, but don't be drawn into that game.

If you impress someone, it's lose-lose. You'll either succeed in impressing them and they'll feel jealous and hate you, or you'll fail in impressing them and they'll consider you a phony. I'm exaggerating, of course, but the tenets of *How to Win Friends and Influence People* by Dale Carnegie are as true today as when the book was written: "Be a good listener. Encourage others to talk about themselves." Listen and learn. Open your mouth, and you'll learn nothing.

There is little reason to impress people and no reason to feel unworthy when you hear of someone else doing well. So force yourself out to meetups, masterminds, and conferences, and go there to listen and learn.

Productivity and focus

Focus is everything to the new breed of entrepreneur. We need to concentrate on what's important despite the distractions of the online world, as well as the plethora of tasks necessary to run a business.

Focus is doubly difficult if you are starting out and not sure of the direction of your business.

I always make sure I **do one thing every day**. This doesn't sound like much, but bear with me.

For example, when I'm writing a book, I try to write 750 words every day. I'd feel bad if I didn't get at least 400 down. I'll try to get the book done in a month.

Similarly, when I'm making a video course, I try to record a video every day. Editing can be time-consuming, although I outsource the initial editing and then add a few finishing touches afterwards. By the end of a month, I'll try to have a video course ready to sell on a variety of platforms.

I also try to **do one thing every week**. This doesn't sound like much, but bear with me.

Blogging is an incredibly useful practice as it improves your personal brand recognition as well as your writing. So it's an important habit to keep up. I write a blog post every week. I would feel bad if I didn't. This has helped me so much. I also try to post a YouTube video every week.

There are a host of **apps that can help you to stay focused.** For example, you can install the News Feed Eradicator plugin for Chrome, which ensures you can't see the Facebook newsfeed when logged into Facebook. There are apps to block the Internet for a set amount of time like *Freedom*; apps that block just social sites like Anti-Social; apps that block out visual distractions and computer applications that can drain your focus; apps that provide "white noise"; and Chrome extensions such as *Inbox Pause* that pause the email coming in that distract you from the task at hand.

According to *Super Brain* by Rudolph E. Tanzi and Deepak Chopra, **doing different things** and going different places every day will help prevent Alzheimer's and make you more energized and productive.

Walk a different way to work or a different way to the shops every day. Work in different cafes every day. Read a book that isn't "your thing." If someone invites you to something you wouldn't usually be interested in, go.

Self-sabotage

Self-sabotage is common amongst new and old entrepreneurs alike.

Self-sabotage occurs when there is a disconnect between what you are doing and what you want inside. So you find yourself doing any task but the task you should be doing to move your business to where you think you want to it go.

New entrepreneurs, especially, can get easily caught up in the latest money-making scheme (known as the "shiny object syndrome"), then lose their way, and then find another. Before long they've spent months flitting from one project to another without getting anything done.

The antidote to the shiny object syndrome is the age-old "do what you love" mantra. It's easy to say, but sometimes desperately difficult to do.

You can identify self-sabotage when you notice you aren't getting things done. You don't have that sense of achievement throughout the day or even at the end of the day.

When you're caught in this malaise, you need to return to your core values. Here I repeat what I say earlier on in the book:

Prioritize exactly what is important to you. Is it really money that you want, or is it happiness? Is it more possessions you want, or more freedom from your attachment to them? What is happiness to you?

What do you enjoy doing? Can you get paid for doing that? What would you do or have you done for free? This can be your new calling.

What would you do if money weren't necessary?

Self-sabotage takes a strange twist when you add location independence into the mix.

I've witnessed people taking six months off in Chiang Mai to try to get a business off the ground. They try something difficult like an app or a digital product, and they don't have the audience, the experience, or the funds to succeed. This is self-sabotage.

Alternatively, as I explained at the beginning of the book, you can always make money in the new economy by doing some sort of freelance work – you would only have to do a few hours a week to be able to survive in Chiang Mai where the cost of living is so cheap.

And yet some people prefer to take on an absurdly difficult project, which fails, and return to the life they had six months previously. Why pick something so difficult? Why not at least find an alternative way of making money by freelancing?

Could it be that deep down inside they didn't really want it to work?

Make sure you are fully congruent with your decisions and actions. It sounds obvious but, ***make sure you really want to succeed***.

Basic Personal Development Hacks for Happiness

The new freedoms in life and work are useless if you are not free on the inside. Here are several basic hacks to make you feel happier no matter where you are in life.

Watch the thinker

If you've spent any time, as I have, watching the thoughts appear in your mind, you will realize that they bubble up and disappear independently for no reason.

Every one of us has this ongoing mental static – the whirring accompaniment to every waking second of our lives.

These thoughts can be harmful to you. Sometimes my thoughts would turn on me:

> *"When will I get a decent job?"*
> *"Why can't I meet the love of my life?"*
> *"How am I going to pay my bills?"*
> *"What's wrong with me?"*

If any one of us started to speak our thoughts aloud, we'd get locked up pretty quick. If anyone said to you some of the things you think about yourself, you would be extremely hurt. Our thoughts are often negatively judgmental to others as well as ourselves.

You can kill this negative self-talk by being the watcher of your thoughts. Catch yourself thinking negatively, notice it, but don't

berate yourself. Calmly turn your attention to something else –
for example, the present moment.

Meditation

The present moment is all we have. It's the only time we've
ever lived in. The only time there ever has been or ever will be.
Everything that is happening, everything that has happened, and
everything that will ever happen is in the present moment.

Meditation is non-judgmental, present-moment awareness.

Try it now! Wherever you are reading these words, whether
you're sitting down at your desk or standing up reading them on
your phone. Close your eyes for a moment. And, with your eyes
closed, notice the feeling of your feet on the floor, your clothes
on your body, or the air coming into and out of your nose.

You should try to meditate every day.

You will lose concentration. You will find your mind
wandering. When this happens, notice it and do **not** berate
yourself. Instead, calmly turn your attention back to the
sensation of the air coming into and out of your nose.

If you've never meditated before, then only do it for a few
minutes at first. However, as it becomes a daily habit, you'll want
to meditate for longer and longer periods.

You'll enjoy moments of great relaxation as your ability to
concentrate on the present improves.

Inside these moments, you'll find great freedom. Inside these
moments, where you are more deeply connected to yourself and
the universe, you can create a better reality for yourself.

I learn meditation from books where I read something similar to the above. But there are many tools you can use as well. A lot of people use *HeadSpace*.

Affirmations

When you're deeply relaxed, you will connect with yourself on a deeper level, and in those moments, you can make suggestions to yourself.

When you're concentrating on yourself within meditation, you can feel the power in your body – the life force that is the oxygen enriching the blood and giving you energy. It feels good.

You can use this good feeling to good effect. You can make the affirmations you want to realize your dreams. These are my rules of affirmations:

- Affirm when you are feeling really good about yourself in a relaxed and powerful state.
- It's better to affirm something that will help other people, not just yourself.

I find this a helpful and powerful practice. I regularly affirm that my business improves and that I help and inspire more people.

Look after your body

Always try to exercise strenuously at least three times a week, but better yet, every day. This may be difficult when you're traveling, but I usually manage to do something. Yoga is popular among location-independent entrepreneurs because you don't need anything to practice it.

Try to eat better food. Sleep well.

Don't be habitual with any substance (alcohol or other) that isn't nourishing your body. Often, first-time travelers find themselves drinking excessively. Many western cultures dictate you must have a drink when you meet someone. So try to plan physical activities during the day with new friends: "Let's go see that temple or take a hike together." Nights are more challenging. If necessary, tell people you can't drink for health reasons.

Look after your mind

You need all your power, energy, chi, or prana. Here's how you store it up.

- **Avoid negativity.** Avoid negative people. Don't watch the news, game shows, reality shows, chat shows, or really anything on TV – the news is not educating you about the world. It's educating you to fear the world.
- **Avoid arguments about politics, sex, religion, anything.** Don't spend any energy asserting your point of view, and people will soon realize the pointlessness of asserting their opinions on you and move on to their next victim.
- **Avoid blame. Accept bad situations.** Try to improve them rather than blaming yourself or anyone else for them.
- **Avoid complaining. Avoid judgement.**

All suffering comes from our brain's inability to accept the present moment.

Read

Instead of watching TV, you can read. There are plenty of entrepreneurial books you can read. But try to vary the subject matter of your reading. The variety of material will force new neural pathways in the brain and therefore improve your mental abilities.

Practice gratitude

You're working towards personal freedom and helping people. You are an amazing success. Be grateful for it. Be grateful for anything.

Don't worry about money. You're not hungry. Money is just a number in a computer that you'll care little for when you're on your deathbed. What will you care about on your deathbed? Care about that now.

Love yourself

You are not separate from the world. You are not a tiny vessel adrift on the ocean – without control and vulnerable to the waves and the weather. Because everything connects with everything, you are everything you eat, you see, you touch, you listen to; you're everyone you meet and everything you interact with.

So, love everything.

Stop having a go at yourself

Yes, we'd all love to follow our self-imposed rules to the letter. But, you're human. You will err. If you sleep in, get annoyed, eat a burger, or fail in some way, then don't worry.

It happens. It's OK.

Be happy

Whatever you do, make sure it makes you happy. If something seems like a bind, then you'll probably do a bad job, get tired, and give up. I know, we've all got to do things we don't want to do. But we can do everything we can to minimize the bad stuff. Break it up, outsource it, pretend you're happy, even if you aren't.

Conduct your life as though you are successful and happy – it makes a huge difference if you do this. But it's real subtle. Believe in your success and happiness without thinking about it. Try not to make it an ego thing.

Don't get all puffed up when you see some success. Instead, humbly continue to provide better products and services, and keep on trying to improve people's lives.

The New Locations

With the new freedom, you can live and work where you want.

The new freedom can mean working in the local coffee shop or working from home to spend more time with your loved ones. So in a sense, the location is unimportant. However, there are significant "hubs" where location-independent entrepreneurs gather.

This location guide inevitably focuses on areas that are popular with digital nomads. This book is *not* about digital nomadism, which is only a small part of the new freedom. This book is for everybody, some of whom will have no desire or ability to visit these hubs.

One of the many advantages of visiting and working in one of the following hubs, however, is the ability to meet with a huge and growing community of location independent entrepreneurs. Meeting fellow entrepreneurs will always benefit entrepreneurs!

These hubs all have differing advantages, cultures, and communities. Thailand is very cheap and is therefore popular with "newbie" entrepreneurs. Ho Chi Minh City is famous for its startup and coding culture. Hubs in more expensive areas of Latin America are considered to have more serious-minded, US-centric entrepreneurs.

My selection of these hubs is very personal. The discussion of Thailand is relatively long because of my substantial experience there. But I've tried to include all the major hubs from across the world, as well as a few lesser known ones. I apologize if I've missed your favorite hub. If so, get in touch with me, and I'll include it next time.

Thailand

I went to Thailand for the first time over a decade ago. I still remember my first night in Bangkok. It started at 10pm in Khosan Road, a bustling area of backpacker hostels. I remember telling myself, "I've not slept in 36 hours. I'll just pop out and get something to eat then I'll go back to the hostel and sleep." Eight hours later I made it to bed. So began a love affair with Thailand that hasn't ended.

A Thai woman I met that night talked about "farang" men – what she liked about them and what she didn't like about them. I'd already read about the term "farang" in my Lonely Planet book (this was 2003) on the plane there. "Farang" is the name the Thais use to describe someone of European descent.

The following three months consisted of going for long motorbike drives through beautiful scenery, visiting temples, playing a lot of pool, reading, meditating, eating, meeting more beautiful women, and sitting in internet cafes.

But there are other reasons why Thailand is a great place to run an online business in the 2010s.

Thai people

I really hate all forms of journalism and writing that glibly characterises Thailand and Thai culture. I find it simplistic and judgmental. I'll try not to do that here. Although probably I will. I don't like to generalize about people from other countries even when it's positive.

And there's a centuries' old "game" of Europeans judging Asians. Europeans love to compartmentalize. They've been coming to Asia and compartmentalizing it, both intellectually and literally, for many years. I'm not sure that Asians judge or compartmentalize Europeans in the same way.

I'm convinced, as a farang, you'll never really understand Thailand, the people, and its culture. I've known many farang who've been there for over 20 years and married into a Thai family, and they'll all disagree on fundamental points about Thailand.

Thailand is known as the "land of the smiles." You'll certainly notice as soon as you get off the plane that Thai people seem, well, happier than people from other countries. Thailand is female friendly, gay friendly, family friendly, LGBT friendly, and, well, pretty friendly all round.

The country has a well developed tourist sector, and the English language is widely spoken, although the Thais speak their own distinctive version of English.

And then there is the multitude of Thai women who partner with farang men (as well as a small amount of Thai men who partner with farang women). Believe me, there is a lot of western judgment about those, and I'm not going to add to it. It happens.

Not to mention the multitude of Thai women with farang women, as well as Thai men with farang men partnerships. And, while we're at it, there is of course a third sex in Thailand: the ladyboys. There are, inevitably, farang partnerships with them too. Thailand is tolerant. Some foreigners don't like it. Guess what? The Thais are tolerant of them, too.

Dalai Lama XIV — 'Love is the absence of judgment.'

I know I've spent too long in the company of farang when I long for a bit of fun.

Thailand is very cheap by western standards

I remember getting a bowl of noodle soup for $0.25-0.35 in Chiang Rai once. Admittedly, this was in 2002. However, nowadays a bowl of noodle soup in Chiang Mai will set you back $0.80.

And don't be thinking that this is a meager portion of noodle soup. It'll fill you up. You'd be forgiven for not finishing this noodle soup. It'll contain vegetables (cabbage, carrots, garlic, etc.), meat (your choice of beef or pork), and, er, noodles.

To be honest, I'm not the biggest fan of noodles. I find them difficult to eat with chopsticks, and they get a bit boring after a while. The longer I spend in Thailand, the spicier the food I eat. The list is endless. Depending on the restaurant, dishes will set you back $1-3.

It's also readily available. Imagine being hungry past midnight in London or New York. Sure, you could call a pizza. But where else apart from Asia could you buy what could be described as healthy, homemade food that has just been cooked in the small hours of the morning? And, added to that, the person serving you at that time will be smiling and polite, and the place you're buying it at won't be full of menacing drunks.

So, we've established that food is excellent, very cheap, and available at all times. But there's more. You don't have to cook or wash up (unless you enjoy doing such things). You also don't have to clean or wash your own clothes.

Condos (condominiums) exist all over Thailand – indeed, all over Southeast Asia. A condo is halfway between a hotel and a rented apartment. You can pay anywhere between $100-500 a month for an apartment with a bathroom (optional extras would be a balcony, kitchen, Jacuzzi, whatever). Usually, apartments come with 24-hour concierge, and you have to pay extra for water, electricity, and Internet.

On the subject of Internet, you can get local SIM cards and purchase plans from local networks where you can get fast 3G or 4G access to mobile internet for reasonable prices. I get AIS, where I tend to spend around $15 a month for local calls and mobile Internet. This is so much cheaper than the equivalent in the UK, as is broadband.

The Internet speed is good

Internet speeds vary from street to street, from city to city, from country to country. Having said that, Thailand's is pretty good. You only have to cross the border into Cambodia to realize that the Thais have invested wisely in bandwidth.

Cross the border again into Vietnam and China, and you'll find certain sites are censored. Internet censorship is usually not a problem in Thailand, but when it is, it can be circumvented with a Virtual Private Network (VPN).

In the UK, where I'm from, the Internet speed can be quite slow, considering it's one of Europe's largest economies, whereas you can find amazingly fast speeds in Czech Republic and Estonia, for example.

If you've spent time in the Philippines, you'll appreciate Thailand's digital infrastructure.

Thailand is a magnet for "digital nomads"

So, it's cheap, welcoming, and friendly, and it has great food, great weather, and good internet speeds …. For the above reasons (and much more), Thailand attracts a good amount of farang.

The most recent farang immigrant to make a beeline for Thailand is the "digital nomad." A digital nomad is an individual who works online and can live anywhere in the world – as long as they have their laptop and access to the Internet.

They're not all farang, of course. There are Asian digital nomads, but the majority of digital nomads are originally from Europe, the Americas, or Australasia.

Working in close proximity to other location-independent entrepreneurs is a double-edged sword. It's great to discuss online business, get ideas, and form mutually beneficial business relationships. On the other hand, hanging out with young male farang gets boring after a while and stops you from exploring the culture of the host country.

Thailand is very safe

I leave my laptop and phone out in a cafe when I go to the restroom. In Thailand, everyone leaves their bike helmets on their bikes. Even if you leave something behind, like a bag in a restaurant, everything is always there where you left it.

One of the first ways to access the new freedom is to avoid the media (television news, online news, and print media), particularly from your home country. The media is only concerned with spreading fear as that is what gives it power. Ignore all western media reports of safety in foreign countries.

Neighboring countries may not be as safe as Thailand, but still, if you employ common sense practices, you'll be fine.

Bangkok, Thailand

Thailand's capital is home to more than 10 million people, gleaming high-rise apartment blocks, traditional neighborhoods, modern shopping malls, and bad traffic.

When in Bangkok, make the use of the fact you don't work nine-to-five and avoid the roads during rush hour. That aside, Bangkok has fantastic and cheap transport: buses and trains, as well as car and motorbike taxis.

I've lived in condos fairly centrally near Thong Lo and Ekkamai along the BTS sky-train stations. On Nut is also popular. Here you can find good accommodations from $400+ per month.

Although it is a tad more expensive than the rest of the country, Bangkok provides a thriving community of location-independent entrepreneurs, as well as a robust local business community.

Bangkok boasts all the amenities and nightlife of a modern metropolis with nearly the same friendliness of elsewhere in the Land of Smiles.

Bangkok Digital Nomad Facebook group: *www.facebook.com/groups/1497047133843898*

Chiang Mai, Thailand

Chiang Mai is Thailand's "second city," although with a population of around 400,000, it's tiny compared to the nation's capital. It's the most culturally important city of northern Thailand and the former capital of the Lanna kingdom, which boasts a slightly different culture, language, and cuisine to the rest of Thailand.

Chiang Mai is home to perhaps the largest community of "digital nomads" in the world – not all of them, but most, are young, single new arrivals. There are older people, families, and entrepreneurs from the rest of Thailand and Asia here, as well as veteran farang with decades of Asian business experience. Chiang Mai is where I've spent most of my time these last two years.

It's one of the cheapest cities in Southeast Asia. It is possible to rent an apartment for US$100 a month here. It is not unreasonable to live in Chiang Mai for less than $500 a month. Many locals, after all, live on much less.

Given the cheap cost of living, modern Internet, and amenities – and, not to mention, ease of living – Chiang Mai has become notorious for "bootstrapping," location-independent entrepreneurs. If you have a business going through an "incubation" period, this could be the place to lengthen that period.

Yet despite these apparently perfect conditions for location-independent entrepreneurs to flourish, Chiang Mai is a big enough city to get lost in. Most digital nomads gravitate towards the trendy Nimman area to the northwest of the old city. Avoid that area, and you can be immersed in the authentic northern Thailand. And, in Chiang Mai and its surroundings, you are never far away from a coffee shop with wifi and electrical outlets, usually air-conditioned. There are also co-working spaces, if that's your thing, with the two branches of Punspace being the most popular.

You may want to get a scooter in Chiang Mai to get around (from $100/month). If not, you could get around by foot if you live and work in the same neighborhood. Or there are songthaews (large trucks with two rows of seats in the back) and tuk-tuks (three wheeled motor-driven rickshaw taxis), but these have their limitations and aren't always available at night.

The one blot on the landscape is the smog that descends upon the city around February to April. This is the result of a centuries' old agricultural burning practice in the area, and it varies from year to year in duration and severity. It's cleared by the rainy season, which usually begins in April. Some people decide to vacate the region during this time.

Chiang Mai Digital Nomads Facebook group: *www.facebook.com/ groups/cmnomads/*

Pai, Thailand

Pai is a small town, 150 km northeast of Chiang Mai (on a beautiful road with 762 bends). It was once a quiet town, but has recently become a tourist destination with many souvenir shops, guesthouses, cafes, and bars, catering to backpackers with many treks, waterfalls, elephant camps, and spas nearby.

Why am I mentioning it? Pai has a small community of location-independent entrepreneurs making the most of the slow pace of life and the unusually fast pace of Internet. Prices are similar to Chiang Mai.

The islands and the south

Islands such as Koh Samui, Koh Phangan, Koh Tao, Koh Lanta, and Phuket, as well as the Krabi area, are more famous as tourist destinations. Prices are higher than in Chiang Mai, but staying long term can be reasonable enough. Rents (usually of bungalows) would be around $400-600 per month. Food is a bit more expensive.

It's harder to find air-conditioned cafes to work from, if that's your thing. But there are no shortage of cafes and restaurants with decent wifi (again mobile 3G/4G will be ample back-up). Some islands, such as Phuket, Koh Tao, and Koh Phangan, have co-working spaces.

Koh Lanta Digital Nomads Facebook group: *www.facebook.com/groups/KohLantaDigitalNomads*

Koh Lanta Locals Facebook group: *www.facebook.com/groups/lantalocals/*

Koh Samui digital nomads Facebook group: *www.facebook.com/groups/824117910967965/*

Koh Phangan digital nomads Facebook group: *www.facebook. com/groups/kpdigitalnomads*

Koh Tao digital nomads Facebook group: *www.facebook.com/ groups/1408505179466597/*

Krabi digital nomads Facebook group: *www.facebook.com/groups/ krabidigitalnomads*

Phnom Penh, Cambodia

Cambodia was in the headlines for all the wrong reasons in decades past. You sometimes feel, after crossing the border from Thailand, that Cambodia is about 30 years "behind" in terms of economic development. However, it's economy has been growing at well over 5% every year since the mid-90s, so it's catching up fast.

I've been to Cambodia's second city, Siem Reap, which is next door to the famous Angkor Wat, as well as Sihanoukville, a city near the tourist beaches and islands. But for me, the best place to work and live is the capital, Phnom Penh.

Phnom Penh boasts co-working spaces and the best Internet connectivity in the country (again, a 4G mobile SIM bought from the airport would be a good back-up), and it lacks the power outages that can affect the rest of the country.

It's a sprawling city of 1.5 million inhabitants that sits at the junction of the Mekong and Tonlé Sap rivers. You could start by looking for a place near the riverfront, which is lined with parks, restaurants, and bars.

You can get a nice apartment for $300-600 per month. Most people, especially young people, speak English and are friendly.

Although crime is reputedly an issue, mainly bag snatching, I didn't feel particularly at risk.

Weather is great during the high season of November to February when it's not too hot or humid. It can be slightly uncomfortable during the wet season.

Phnom Penh & Expat Forum: *www.facebook.com/groups/phnompenhexpatforum/*

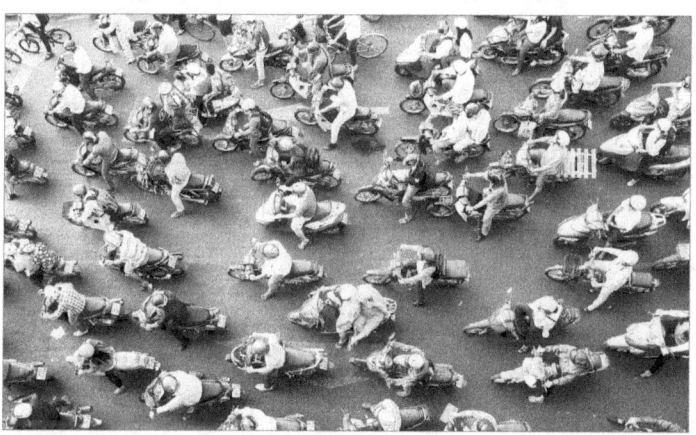

Ho Chi Minh City, Vietnam

Formally known as Saigon, Ho Chi Minh City is Vietnam's largest city with over 9 million inhabitants. Ho Chi Minh still shows the signs of French colonial architecture with Chinese and American influences. Ho Chi Minh is a bustling, confusing, scooter-populated metropolis with modern skyscrapers, Oriental style pagodas, and an abundance of street food stalls.

In terms of weather, it's always warm here, ranging from 31C (88F) in December to 34C (94F) in April, so plan your visit based on avoiding the rainy season. December to April are driest, with about three rainy days each.

The city is second to Chiang Mai in terms of an Asian digital nomad destination or maybe an equal second with Bali.

The most popular district for new arrivals is 18A where you can get short leases for $300-500/month. Longer term leases are a better value for the money elsewhere in the city where $500/month will get you a great three-bedroom apartment.

Coffee shops abound in HCMC, so you won't be short of places to work in. There are co-working spaces as well. Check out Dreamplex, which is the most popular and was visited by President Obama in 2016.

Crime is more of a problem here compared to Thailand and is on the rise, but it is still much lower than in the west. Women and vulnerable male drunks seem to be the biggest targets.
The Hoch Coach: *www.facebook.com/groups/1534183903495652*
Saigon Digital Nomads Facebook group: *www.facebook.com/groups/saigonnomads*
Dreamplex: *www.facebook.com/dreamplexvn*

Cebu, Philippines

The Philippines is a popular destination for location-independent entrepreneurs. The local low wages and high English fluency make this a good place to recruit and build teams for your business.

Prices are reasonable. In Cebu, an unfurnished studio in IT Park starts at $200 per month with a minimum lease of six months. You have to pay two months' rent as a deposit and one month of your rent in advance. Pay $200-300 more, and you'll get a separate bedroom and balcony. Air-conditioned taxis are easy to find and usually fairly cheap. Cheaper still are the ubiquitous Filipino Jeepneys, which follow set routes and aren't air-conditioned.

The Internet in the Philippines isn't good. You can get high speeds and fibre in co-working spaces and a tiny amount of places in the center of large towns. Other than that, it's sometimes frustrating.

Crime is also an issue in the Philippines. The Philippines may have more crime against foreigners than Thailand, and many banks and malls are protected by armed security guards. However, if you stick to the central tourist areas of Manila, Cebu, and Davao, as well as the resorts, and use your common sense, you will be fine.

Cebu is the Philippines "second city," although the fifth in terms of population, which is nearly one million. (Metro Cebu is three million.) Weather in Cebu ranges from a 30C (85F) in May to 27C (81F) in January. It does rain often in Cebu, with every other or every third day involving a shower, depending on the season. Make note to avoid June to October because it's typhoon season. Typhoons can sometimes be dangerous, and they most certainly will keep you locked up indoors and temporarily ruin the beautiful beaches and nature you'll want to visit. There are many resorts and dive spots accessible, although traffic in central Cebu is pretty bad at rush hour.

The best wifi can be had in the Marriott, an expensive hotel in the center of town, but you can sit in the lobby and use it for the price of a coffee. There are plenty of places to work in the neighboring Ayala Center, but with the usual sluggish Filipino wifi. One of the most popular co-working places is the Tide in Cebu IT Park, which is a mixed-use business park in the center of the city.

The Tide: *www.facebook.com/TheTIDECebu/*

Cebu digital nomads: *www.facebook.com/groups/cebudigitalnomads/*

Manila and Davao are also popular hubs for location-independent entrepreneurs in the Philippines. Davao has similar prices to Cebu but with less traffic congestion. Manila, the capital, is more expensive and is infamous for its traffic jams.

Davao Digital Nomads: *www.facebook.com/groups/oDeskDavao/*

Bali, Indonesia

Bali is just one of Indonesia's 13,466 islands, but probably the most famous. 4.2 million inhabitants spread themselves along its shores. Indonesia is home to many religions – Islam, Christianity, Hindu, and Buddhism, to name a few. The prevalence of different religions tends to vary from island to island. Bali happens to be 82% Hindu. Home to the world's highest biodiversity and a great location for diving, Bali's daily highs are between 30-34C (86-93F) year round, so when you are deciding on when to visit, choose its dry season of April to September.

Costs vary widely in Bali. Living and eating out like a local actually costs very little (~$2 per meal), but many of the expats find themselves caving into extras – $3 on artisan coffees, $10 for yoga or other activities, $8 on an organic salad. That said, if you can resist such luxuries, you can still afford to live there for a reasonable cost. Accommodation can be found for as low as $300 a month and can go upwards to $1100 for those willing to splurge. Ubud has far and away the largest digital nomad scene and is often compared with Chiang Mai in terms of popularity and liveability. Unlike Chiang Mai, however, negotiating good internet is much more difficult in Bali, which makes going to a co-working space more of a priority.

To find a place to live, use the newspaper (yes, the classifieds) or go around and pound the pavement. It's generally preferred to rent somewhere peaceful, like the centre of a rice paddy, and then get a scooter ($60/month with petrol) to get around.

Use the ATMs of Permata and BI to avoid ATM fees, and make sure to get into the "visa on arrival" line at the airport **before** passing through immigration. $35 will extend your ability to stay in Indonesia from 30 to 60 days, should you decide to stay, and this cannot be done afterwards without flying in and out of the country again.

There are far fewer backpackers in Bali than in other Asian hubs. Rather, location-independents in their 30s abound. Hubud is Ubud's most popular co-working hub and full of ambitious globetrotters. It is also the most pricey at roughly $1 per hour.

Bali Digital Nomads Facebook group: *www.facebook.com/groups/ balidigitalnomads*
Hubud: *www.hubud.org*

Barcelona, Spain

Spain has long been Europe's escape from the cold, and Barcelona is a particular favorite for all those who have had it with their own countries. Due to modern changes in working arrangements, its 1.6 million inhabitants have seen a steady growth in location-independents working and living side-by-side with the locals, and it's generally possible to get around with English. Winters are a relaxing 14C (59F), and summers top out at 29C (84F).

Rent relative to other costs is very cheap in Barcelona. A one-bedroom will set you back $775 in the centre, $600 outside of it. Add another $170 for electric, water, and internet. Meals at lower cost restaurants average $12, and a beer can be had for around $3. You'll probably want to consider cooking while here.

When not working, you'll want to spend your days walking around this beautiful city and your nights overlooking the water at the harbor. Be extremely mindful of your belongings – Barcelona and Rome compete for the world's most competent pickpockets. Put your wallet in your front pocket, leaving excess cards and IDs locked up if you can, and split cash between less than $20 in a front pocket and more stashed away. Never take your hands (not just your eyes) off your laptop. With that said, you will love it here. When you've had enough of the night cafes and wines, take a weekend trip out to the nearby mountains for a hike.

Barcelona has so many co-working spaces that it is impossible to list them all there. Visit Barcelona Navigator to see photos and brief description of each, and choose somewhere that fits with your tastes and location: *barcelonanavigator.com/barcelona-co-working-spaces/*

Connect with other of Barcelona's location-independents through Facebook groups or using Meetup.com.

Barcelona Location Independent Professionals: *www.facebook.com/groups/847138072058478*

Barcelona Entrepreneurs and Digital Nomads: *www.facebook.com/groups/847138072058478*

Codio - Communit of Digital Nomads: *www.meetup.com/codino/*

Berlin, Germany

Berlin is a city unlike any other. It's 3.6 million inhabitants aren't much impressed by the well dressed. It has a thriving cafe culture and night scene. Berlin isn't what you'd call a pretty city, as the majority of it was levelled in the last World War. It is, however, chock full of museums, and history, which the Germans have on open display as a reminder to the world against fascism. This is a city where you'll find everyone being exactly who they want to be. Winters rest right around freezing at 0C (32F), and summers peak at 24C (75F). Unlike the rest of Germany, Berliners speak excellent English.

Its cheap rents, as well as city planning, has attracted a huge number of startups in recent years, so prices have risen. But a one-bedroom in the city center is still manageable at $750 or $530, if you choose to live outside the city. Utilities are a significant added cost, however. Expect around $250 a month on top of rent. Eating out can be had for around $8.80, coffee for $2.80, and a German beer for $3.30.

The digital nomad "scene" is centered around the trendy Kreuzberg area of town, which has emerged from its history as one of the poorest quarters in the old West Berlin to one of the cultural centers of the now reunified city. Here you can find co-working spaces, such as Betahaus, which has a small cafe area where you can work for free, as well as larger, quieter spaces with fast Internet. Internet speeds around the city are generally excellent.

Betahaus Berlin: *www.betahaus.com/berlin/*

Berlin Digital Nomads Facebook group: *www.facebook.com/ groups/berlindigitalnomads/*

Prague, Czech Republic

Prague is arguably Europe's most beautiful city. As a European center of economics, culture, and politics through the Gothic, Renaissance, and Baroque periods, it is flourishing with history, sites, and museums. You'll find yourself stunned by the statues decorating the bridges. It features a castle overlooking the city, which was first built in 850AD. It is a smallish capital city, with just over one million inhabitants. The location-independent entrepreneurs, unlike in Berlin, are slightly spread out over the city. There are plenty of co-working spaces, again, spread out over the city center (which isn't that big).

English is widely spoken in this central European city, and the winters teeter upon freezing during the months of December and January, with highs averaging 18C (64F) in July.

Living in Prague is considered quite affordable. One-bedroom apartments can be had for $580 in the city centre and $420 outside of it. Budget $170 for utilities and $22 for a monthly transit pass. Eating out starts at $5, and beers (which you *have* to drink in

Prague) at $1.50. Taxis are reasonable and easy to pick up.

Internet won't be a problem. Prague is one of the best cities for Internet connectivity. Most of the cafes have fast wifi – they usually don't even bother to password protect it.

Prague digital nomads: *www.facebook.com/groups/prague. digitalnomads*

Sarajevo, Bosnia

Sarajevo lies on a European cultural faultline and is sometimes referred to as the Jerusalem of Europe. Historically, it's the place where the Roman empire split, leaving Catholics populating the east, Orthodox peoples in the west, and the Ottomans in the south. This resulted in wars and clashes at the time and gave way to a modern-day practice of tolerance and diversity. 400,000 Bosnians call this capital home, and importantly, it is very safe. Sarajevo is not, however, warm. With its July highs at 19C (66F) and January just two degrees below zero (28F), it is best to come between May and September to enjoy good weather and the least amount of rain.

Rent in Sarajevo is very affordable. Depending on the season and how much effort you put in, flats can be found for as low as $80 a month on up to $200. Wifi can be found at many of the cafes, and local meals will cost between $1.50 to $5, depending on what and how locally you eat. If you like meat, you are in for something special. Try the local evapi (meat in pita bread with onions) for $3, a steak or mali biftek for $2-4, or one of the many varieties of Sarajevo's meat and vegetable pies.

The locals love their coffee, and their cafes often turn into bars at nighttime. Just don't be surprised to see the locals still drinking coffee at 9pm. There are also plenty of underground clubs and such, if you like. Use a quick Internet search when you get there to find which are still operating.

Sarajevo does not have the cheapest flights, so take a bus from Berlin or one of the other major cities nearby if you are economizing.

In terms of working and networking, you'll find plenty of other entrepreneurs and locationally challenged individuals at Nest71. *www.nest71.com*

Malmo, Sweden

Malmo is a bit of an unorthodox choice. Located a short 40-minute train ride from the Copenhagen airport, Malmo is Sweden's third largest city. It's more expensive than other options and not traditionally known as a nomad spot. What it does have, however, is a thriving startup scene. Flooded with technical talent ranging from programmers from Malmo University to ex-Sony Mobile engineers, the city has abundant creativity and a welcoming entrepreneurial community.

Visiting in summer is recommended; otherwise, renting in Sweden can be tricky. Housing is scarce, and while Malmo has much more available than the Swedish capital of Stockholm, it's still a pain. While there is some avilability on AirBnB, you can also try this Swedish-language accommodation site: *kvalster.se/Malmo* and use Chrome or Google to translate into English. Try to pick up a sublet of a one bedroom ($800/month) or a private room ($400/month) for your stay.

Summertime, particularly June 15th to August 15th, is a great time to visit. Apartments are readily available as students are home or vacationing abroad, and the local transport pass (Jojo Kort) can be had at a reduced $75 during this exact period – it will get you unlimited travel around the entire region/state of Skane.

Expect to do a lot of cooking, as eating out is expensive in Sweden. Lunch can be had for around $11, but street food such as falafel or kebabs abound at $3-5.

Spend your weekends visiting a lot of little cities in the region of Skane. Say "hi" to people on the buses, and ask them a question about the place you want to go. They are most likely doing the same, and this is an easy way to make friends. Check out this website for all the free summer events in the city: *www.malmotown.com/en/article/summer-events/*

Malmo airport also has cheap flights as low as $10 to many central european countries via Wizz Air if you book a few weeks in advance.

Foo Cafe and Minc are great places to both work and to meet other ambitious entrepreneurs. You'll be amazed at the sheer range of activities and industries this community has budding in it.

Foo Cafe: *www.foocafe.org*

Minc: *www.minc.se*

Øresund Startup News: *www.facebook.com/oresundstartups*,

Malmö Startups: *www.facebook.com/groups/malmostartups/*.

Medellin, Colombia

Known as the City of Eternal Spring, Medellin maintains a year round temperate 28°C. You might associate this Colombian city of 2.2 million inhabitants with its violent past and Pablo Escobar, but now this is far from the truth. Decades of investment into urban planning earned this country "the most innovative city in the world" title in 2013, and Medillin ties for first place as the best city to live in South America.

Accommodations with utilities won't set you back much. Flats slightly outside the city center can be found fully furnished for $500 a month, or $300 will get you a studio.

The social life of Medellin is vibrant. There's something to do every night, and you'll find the Colombian people warm and welcoming. You'll quickly find yourself feeling at home.

If you've never tried it before, private classes in Salsa or Spanish start around $4, and with a few steps you'll be well on your way to meeting the locals.

A plethora of co-working spaces can be found all across the city. The metro systems are world class, and if you need to get away from it all, a 30-minute ride will take you up into the breathtaking mountains surrounding the city.

Medellin Digital Nomad Facebook Group: *www.facebook.com/ groups/1659082490994738*

Lima, Peru

The food is fresh from surrounding farms, the city is alive with things to do, and the Peruvian people themselves will capture your heart. Lima's 9.5 million inhabitants enjoy all of the benefits of a coastal city that is nestled between the foothills of nearby mountains. Its beaches and great year-round weather make being outside a joy. The city of Lima receives just 13mm (.5in) of rain each year.

A furnished one-bedroom apartment can be found for around $575 in the city centre and $350 outside the city. A two-month deposit is typically required. Utilities, such as water and Internet, will add $100 to those prices. A metro trip is around $.50 and a monthly pass is $30. Local food runs in the range of $3.50 a meal, and your beers will set you back $1.50-2. If uncertain where to rent, Barranco is a good place to start, right off the ocean cliffs.

Like Medellin, co-working spaces can be seen popping up all over the southern and coastal areas of the city, though online meetup groups from the locationally independent aren't as organized. Show up at Co-Working in The Sun and get plugged in from there. And don't worry, you will most certainly make local friends while you are there.

Co-Working in The Sun: *www.facebook.com/coworkinginthesun*

Santiago, Chile

Due to its proximity to the Andes mountains and the Pacific Ocean, those living in Santiago can ski and surf on the same day. Santiago's 6.2 million inhabitants enjoy warm summers (29C/85F) and refreshing winters (14C/58F). Santiago and Chile in general are experiencing rapid growth due to the country's recent crackdown on corruption and progressive investment into startups. Chile is one of South America's least corrupt countries, and its startup program, Start-Up Chile, attracts the best entrepreneurs in the world with free $30,000USD grants and one-year residency visas. You will find no shortage of like-minded individuals living a location-free lifestyle.

Santiago is more expensive than most of Latin America. $7.60 will get you lunch at a local restaurant, and rent is fairly consistent across the city, centre or outskirts. Around $450 will get you a one-bedroom and $880 a three-bedroom. Add approximately $150 a month for utilities and internet. Use Craigslist to find one. A monthly metropass can be had for around $50. Wine is abundantly cheap at around $4 a bottle, and if you like to cook, you can easily thrive off fresh meats and produce for $100 each month.

If skiing or surfing aren't your cup of tea, try the wine! Santiago is surrounded by vineyards for which tours are readily available from the city. As Santiago is also famous for its museum culture, when you find yourself in need of inspiration, your muse is right around the corner.

The majority of co-working spaces are located in the northeastern areas of the city, with Urban Station being the most famous. A membership there will get you access to their multiple locations in Santiago and other South American cities. Visit them in person to get plugged in.

Urban Station: *chile.enjoyurbanstation.com/es/home/*

Central America: Costa Rica and Nicaragua

You can hike volcanoes, go on jungle safaris, rescue turtles, surf, kite surf, white water raft, or just soak up some sunshine in a hammock. Of course, you might also want to do some work. Not to worry, Costa Rica is a "wifi heaven." The weather is also 27C/81F year round.

As in most of Central America, avoid the capital, San Jose. Instead, you'll find many like-minded individuals in Liberia, even more in San Isidro de El General, and, most popularly, in Puerto Viejo. Costa Rica is the most expensive country in Central America with rentals of one-bedrooms averaging $522 in downtown San Jose and around $380 elsewhere. Budget $110 for utilities and internet, and be prepared to pay to eat out. A meal at an inexpensive restaurant can set you back $7.34!

If this seems too expensive to you, head north a few hours to Nicaragua and enjoy all the same activities. Plant yourself in San Juan Del Sur if you love to surf or Granada if you love charming colonial architecture. Costs are generally half of the more developed Costa Rica, but that itself has a cost. Power outages are still a regular occurrence, so be ready to work off your batteries. Keep them charged! Internet can be had via a modem from Claro, which costs $32, and you'll pay an additional $30 for 5GB of 3G internet.

Spanish and Salsa lessons typically run around $5. It pays to take Spanish lesson. While the locals are beyond friendly, English is virtually non existent, particularly in Nicaragua.

Unfortunately, the working independents aren't as organized in these areas, but don't worry. An unlimited supply of coconuts and waves makes everyone friendly. Just say "hi" to people you see with laptops, and you'll make friends soon enough. Be sure to check your desired destination's rainy season before coming. It varies from region to region in each country! Nine months of the year in most of this region is paradise, but the other three often are not.

Costa Rica digital nomad Facebook group: *www.facebook.com/ groups/costaricadigitalnomads*

Austin, Texas

Austin has long been famous as a progressive university oasis and the "live music capital of the world" with the most music venues per capita in the US. Today it also has its own thriving Silicon Valley, or "Silicon Hills," as it's called. Summers are a hot 35C/95F and winters a pleasant 16C/62F.

Rent here is not cheap. Expect to pay at least $1500 in the city center and $1000 outside it. Utilities, including internet, can be $200 extra. Pick up a short-term sublet on craigslist.org or use AirBnb. Restaurant meals are $12 on the low end. So why mention this city? Well, Austin is repeatedly ranked as the best city to live in the US, and in 2016 took first as having the "best people" in terms of personality. This could be due to the city's motto, "Keep Austin Weird," and its resistance against capital and cheap materialism. There is a bus system, and it's one of the few cities in the US where getting around by bike is possible.

Co-working spaces abound, and you'll find a thriving meet up scene of location-independents if you search "digital nomad" or "4-Hour Work Week" in Austin on Meetup.com.

The new location isn't important

In a sense, there is no new location as, with the new freedom, there is no location necessary. You could go to a "hub," you could go on a cruise, or you could stay at home. What matters is that you enjoy yourself.

However, there are a few things that you may want to take with you on your travels – and I'm not just talking about insect repellent and sunscreen.

Packing Checklist

Traveling forces you into minimalism. Imagine carrying everything you have ever bought! I just carry the essentials. All I need weighs 10kg (22lbs). Many people pack more for a weekend than I do when spending many months on the road. Life is good when it's really simple.

Other people carry more. Those who "settle down" for longer periods in a host country will start amassing more possessions and keep a home base.

There are a few essentials that most people swear by that I've included in this chapter to help you when packing for your next trip. Whether you're planning a few days away or leaving home forever, this is going to help you.

Forgive me as I geek out on the following travel items!

Bag/backpack

Bag, backpack, suitcase ... it doesn't really matter. Long-term travelers tend to favor two backpacks (a big one and a small one), a big bag for possessions (clothes, toiletries, etc.), and a small one (messenger bag) to carry the laptop, power cables, and other daily necessities.

I followed advice from my friend Zach Swinehart and got the Osprey Farpoint 55. The Osprey Farpoint 55 has a zip off daypack, which simplifies things – the small bag zips onto the big bag, so I only have to carry one bag.

Unfortunately, there's no consistency amongst the airlines for the maximum weight and size you are allowed to carry on planes. However, I've always been able to take the above backpack and daypack separately as carry-on luggage. Some low-cost European airlines may not be so lenient.

There are plenty of bags out there that nomads swear by, like the Minaal and the Tortuga, or brands such as Deuter, Jansport, Timbuk2, and Northface, for example. And I'm sure many people prefer suitcases with wheels and other options.

You can find links to backpacks mentioned in this section as well as links to many other products listed in this book's resources page at *robcubbon.com/kindle8*.

Packing clothes, shoes, toiletries, towels, and numerous tech accessories into a backpack can mean strenuous forcing of the zips to squeeze everything in, and then the inevitable "backpack explosion" when unpacking at your destination.

This is where products such as packing cubes, compression sacks, the Hoboroll, and pack tubes come into play. These products are essentially packs within backpacks that compress and organize items within your luggage to simplify and save space.

Laptop

The most expensive piece of the kit you'll be taking is the most important. It's a hugely personal choice, so there's no point in saying much about it here. Other than the most important points: make sure the laptop's files and software are backed-up both on the cloud and on a physical external drive you have with you. And make sure it's password protected.

I have a MacBook Pro (Retina, 15-inch, Late 2013) maxed out to 16GB RAM and 1TB of flash storage. It allows me to zip through high resolution video editing and Photoshop work. I put stickers on it. I figure a laptop that looks beat-up and unloved is less likely to be stolen.

Laptop accessories: laptop stands are an answer to neck ache. The Roost Stand is popular. And some people like to take a portable keyboard and mouse, as the laptop's keyboard and trackpad have their limitations.

Phone

Again, this is another essential, expensive item that is a personal decision, so I won't say much here. I prefer Samsung Android phones, others prefer the iPhone variety. I like the larger phone since it doubles up as a tablet reading device.

The most important point about your phone is to, again, make sure it's password protected. And I prefer to own a phone and unlock it so I can use cheap local SIM cards for calls and data.

Phone accessories: as the phone is an important piece of kit, you may want to invest in a cover for the screen and a case to prevent damage if dropped. Some phone cases double as chargers and can give you maybe 25% more battery life.

SIM card

There are three reasons why you'd possess multiple SIM cards: you're either a criminal, an adulterer, or a location-independent entrepreneur.

The cheapest way to use a phone while traveling is to have it unlocked and buy pay-as-you-go SIMs to give you cheap local calls and 3G or 4G access. The more you travel, the more SIM cards you pick up. So you'll need somewhere to put them, and remember where that is, as these tiny things get lost easily. Newer smartphones have the ability to house two SIMs, and you can switch between the two without physically changing them.

One carrier for the frequent traveler is ChatSim. For just $10 a year, you can get a steady phone number on which you can receive texts (important for your authentications to Facebook, Google, PayPal, etc) and unlimited text-based messaging on the most popular apps in almost every country in the world: Facebook Messenger, WhatsApp, LINE, WeChat, Kik, etc. For a few extra dollars, you can use it for some phone calls or for emergency internet browsing.

Another option is *Project Fi* from Google, which seamlessly switches your phone from one network to another anywhere in the world, always giving you the strongest signal at a reasonable price. The downside to this is that you must have a Nexus 5 or higher. This is currently being used by constant traveler Matt Mullenweg, founding developer of WordPress and CEO of Automattic, a company of over 500 employees who all work remotely.

External drive

External drives are recommended for handy physical back-up.

I have a WD Elements 2TB USB Passport portable hard drive. I have this partitioned into two drives. One backs up my work with Mac's TimeMachine; and the other contains disc images of software I use regularly, so if something stops working, I can reinstall.

Earphones

Earphones are a "must" for working remotely. Earphones are useful for Skype chats, Blabs, podcast interviews, and Hangouts. They are also useful for listening to music, Google Maps directions, and for blocking out the world to focus on what you're doing.

Bose QuietComfort and other noise-canceling earphones are recommended by regular travelers. This is because the noise canceling "turns the world off" – you will not hear the noise of the aircraft you're traveling on, and you are free to enjoy the music or concentrate on the podcast you are listening to without any distractions.

Adapters, power cables, and battery packs

Initially you will bring one adapter for each of your devices. But some travel chargers plug in multiple devices from one power outlet and provide power protection from damaging voltage surges.

Portable battery packs are recommended to keep your phone alive for long periods or on long-haul flights.

Video and audio recording

Due to the nature of online business, traveling entrepreneurs are often making videos, taking photos, or recording audio. For this reason, we're constantly looking for quality audio and video tech that is also lightweight and easily portable.

Great video and photos can be taken with modern iPhone and Samsung mobiles. However, there are accessories that you also need.

For example, I find a table tripod useful to travel around with. At under three bucks this is a seriously cheap bit of kit. You need to make sure you have the mount for your phone to screw onto this tripod. Then you can take great quality movies of yourself with your phone.

There are two types of microphone I take with me. The first is a lapel mic for doing to-camera videos. I'm told that the best one is the Audio Technica Omni Lav mic. The second mic I use is the

Samson Meteor because of its portability over the Blue Yeti. Both these mics require pop filters. Sometimes a sock pulled over a microphone can double as a pop filter.

Justin Cooke, website broker and co-host of the successful EmpireFlippers podcast, travels with the Audio-Technica ATR-2100 podcast microphone. When recording podcast episodes or doing interviews on the road, he uses that mic and a "pillow fort" (a pillow fort is like a pretend structure that kids make from pillows, sheets, and blankets, and is also good for acoustics). You can read an interview with Justin Cooke at the end of the book.

> Links to all the products listed here, as well as others, can be found on this book's resources page at *robcubbon.com/ kindle8*.

Other stuff to take

Don't worry too much about items (clothes and toiletries, for example) that you can buy very cheaply at the destination country. Even though I'm getting more and more minimal and my luggage weighs less than 10kg, I still find stuff at the bottom of the bag that I've never used.

However, there are a few more essentials.

There's the passport, for instance – you wouldn't get too far without that.

You don't get too far without money, either. I strongly recommend having at least two cards you can withdraw money with, and leave the second locked up at your hotel or residence.

So if one is eaten by an ATM, blocked, or in the worst case, pickpocketed, you will never be without access to cash.

Whenever possible, keep your passport locked up as well once you arrive at your hotel or apartment. Take of a photo of the ID page and the page of your entry stamp, save it to the cloud, and carry around a printed copy of these pages as well, just in case the police stop you for some reason.

Other items regular travelers carry:

- Pens and paper.
- Ear plugs and eye mask for sleeping on flights. Jodi Ettenburg from LegalNomads.com mentions specifically Spark-Plug earplugs.
- Medication.
- Natural protein bars (Quest Nutrition), cashew/Brazilian/ other nuts, and food supplements, especially those that enhance your immune system.

The new traveling

Open-ended traveling while working is one of the best things I've ever done. Nothing beats the feeling of driving a motorcycle into the unknown with your possessions on your back, when you can go anywhere you want, for as long as you want, and still get paid.

It is doable for multitudes of people, they just don't know it yet. You don't need to be rich, male, young, western, able-bodied, or even particularly intelligent to do this. You just need desire.

Interviews

Avery Breyer

 Avery Breyer (*AveryBreyer.com*) is a multiple best-selling author and freelance writer who has been living as a digital nomad with her family for over two years. Avery writes about personal finance and home-based business. She's been seen in/on multiple media outlets, including Woman's World magazine, Time.com, MSN Money, Nasdaq.com, GoBanking Rates, and live radio in New York.

After nearly two years in Southeast Asia, this Canadian family is currently living in Mexico. Avery started from scratch, building a new career for herself to enable her location-independent lifestyle, and believes that if she can do it, anyone can.

What were the first steps you took towards location independence and a more flexible work life?

I started researching ways to earn money online. I wasn't interested in minimum wage work, though, because I have a family and was used to earning good money for my time in my old career. I needed to find something that would earn me enough to live a comfortable life, anywhere I wanted.

How has this helped your life?

I love the freedom of being able to work where and when I want. I have a passion for traveling, and the restrictions on vacation time in our old life didn't suit me. I know that may make me sound spoiled, but the way I see it is if something in your life isn't suiting you, figure out a way to make it better. And that's what location independence has done for me. It solved my travel restriction problem.

How has this helped your business?

I have nothing to compare it to. Like most people, prior to building my location independent income streams, I was an employee at a job that was not suitable for remote work - I had to physically be there. The industry I was in required you to be physically present. So my only choice if I wanted to be location independent was to reinvent myself and find something completely different to do for a living.

What have you found the most challenging aspect of travelling or remote working, and how are you combatting it?

I'm a planner. I have plan A, B, C, D, E, F, G etc. I think that's helped me to avoid any truly horrible things happening to us while traveling. So, honestly, the worst thing that's ever happened to me was a gastrointestinal illness in Vietnam, which, although it wasn't fun to endure, was easily treatable.

Aside from the phone, earphones, laptop, external drive, chargers, clothes, toiletries, credit cards, and passport, what stuff do you always pack that you couldn't do without?

Eye drops. I literally travel with two full-size carryon suitcases full of eyedrops. I have severe eye problems induced by LASIK surgery many years ago, and cannot function without those very specific brands of eye drops. And since I never know ahead of time if they'll be available for purchase in the countries I'm traveling to (most of the time, they're not), I have no choice but to pack a full year's worth to bring with me. (We travel for 10 months, then visit home for two months... then repeat... I bring two months extra of my drops in case I arrive home and find out they're on backorder.)

Aside from Google Drive and other main cloud-based services, what is one online application you couldn't do without?

Lastpass for password management, and Crashplan to backup my computer into the cloud. Both are lifesavers.

What other tools, team members, or tasks do you employ to keep your business working well?

I've experimented with hiring others to do my book covers via 99designs and outsourcing my SEO writing work via UpWork. But most of the time, I'm a one-woman show and do everything myself.

What advice would you give someone who wants to add greater location independence, freedom, and flexibility to their lives?

You have to hustle your butt off, be persistent, and refuse to give up until you've found the business model that works for you. There's a world of opportunity out there for the hustlers and go-getters. And don't believe for one second that "get rich quick" is real. It's not. Anyone I know who's rocking their online biz paid their dues to get there. But the good news is, if they can do it, so can you.

Also, be open-minded when opportunities come your way, and invest in yourself to get the training you need to learn new skills (although be careful who you give your money to, since not all online trainings are created equal). Online courses have a bad rap, there's a lot of garbage out there. However, that doesn't mean that there isn't gold hidden in there too - you just have to find the right person to teach you what you need to know. I wouldn't be where I am today if I hadn't bought courses from the right people to learn the things I needed to know.

Nathan Segal

Canadian Nathan Segal has been a freelance writer for 17 years. In 2004, he went to Mexico on holiday. The following year after a relationship breakup, he went back to the town in Mexico where he'd stayed the previous year. This sparked years of travel back and forth between Canada and Mexico. His work (now book publishing) is done online, allowing him the freedom to travel while working.

Read more about Nathan at *nathansegal.info* and *TravelswithNathan.com*.

What were the first steps you took towards location independence and a more flexible work life?

I bought a laptop with WiFi, made sure I was vaccinated for tetanus, as well as hepatitis A and B, and I took antibiotic medication with me, along with medicine for malaria. I also made sure my passport was current and that I had backups of all my valuable computer information. I bought a portable surge suppressor to protect my electronics from power spikes as I traveled. I also bought an unlocked cell phone, so I could install chips from any country I visited.

How has this helped your life?

This allows me to travel with the essentials covered and work from anywhere there is an Internet connection. I've been doing this for 12 years now.

How has this helped your business?

I've gone beyond what most people have done. I built all my businesses online, so I don't have to work in any specific location.

Aside from the phone, earphones, laptop, external drive, chargers, clothes, toiletries, credit cards, and passport, what stuff do you always pack that you couldn't do without?

A toolkit for my laptop, making sure my phone is unlocked, plenty of currency for the country where I'm going to travel, and emergency numbers in place in case of trouble.

Aside from Google Drive and other main cloud-based services, what is one online application you couldn't do without?

Not so much an application as a service. High Speed WiFi and access to my email and bank accounts.

What other tools, team members, or tasks do you employ to keep your business working well?

MS Office, Camtasia Studio, an iRIG MIC HD for recordings. I don't have team members – yet.

What advice would you give someone who wants to add greater location independence, freedom, and flexibility to their lives?

Stop trying to get everything right. Inevitably, you're going to miss something, maybe several somethings. If you want to find out how life really works, talk to the locals through forums and groups. Don't listen to mainstream media much. There's a lot of disinformation there. The locals are your best bet. Trust your gut when you travel, and be open to adventure. Be willing to explore and ask lots of questions. If you're traveling to a foreign country, make an effort to learn the language. Not only will it help with your journey, chances are the locals will respect you more. Learning the language can open the doors to opportunities that might not exist if you only stick with English (or whatever your native language is).

Akash Karia

Akash Karia (*www.akashkaria.com*) is an international bestselling author, speaker, and consultant. He has coached over 120,000 people worldwide, from bankers in Hong Kong to government members in Dubai to sales executives in Switzerland. He helps individuals and teams craft powerful stories, deliver persuasive presentations, and increase sales conversions.

What were the first steps you took towards location independence and a more flexible work life?

Since the age of 12, I knew I wanted to write a book. I loved reading books. I was the kid who would spend my lunchtimes in the library reading, so the desire to write a book of my own felt natural to me.

I bought my first Kindle when I was in university. I realized that I was spending too much money on buying physical books from bookstores, so buying a Kindle was a way to access cheaper books (and save more money). While reading Kindle books, I thought "Wouldn't it be cool to publish a Kindle book and have millions of people reading it?"

I started researching how to write and publish a Kindle book, and after an entire year of toil and sweat, I published my book, *Speak Like a Winner..* I made less than a $100 in the first month. But I was **excited**. So I published my second book, *How to Deliver a Great TED Talk* - which did phenomenally well and has now been translated into three different languages.

How has this helped your life?

I have written over 15 books - some have been **very** popular, others haven't taken off as well as I hoped. But writing has allowed me to quit my full-time job and make a living doing what I love.

Furthermore, I'm also a global keynote speaker and travel around the world giving workshops and seminars. My #1 source of leads? My books!

How has this helped your business?

80% of my speaking leads come from books.

What have you found the most challenging aspect of travelling or remote working, and how are you combatting it?

The most challenging aspect is keeping myself disciplined. With no set working hours and no one to monitor my work, I need to ensure that I'm spending the day productively instead of wasting time/taking things too easy. Just because you are able to make a living online doesn't mean that you can sit back and be lazy...if you stop working, soon your income source will dry up!

Aside from the phone, earphones, laptop, external drive, chargers, clothes, toiletries, credit cards, and passport, what stuff do you always pack that you couldn't do without?

My Kindle so I can read.

Aside from Google Drive and other main cloud-based services, what is one online application you couldn't do without?

I use an application called Expense to keep track of my income and expenses.

What other tools, team members, or tasks do you employ to keep your business working well?

As simple as it sounds, the #1 productivity tool I use is a to-do list.

What advice would you give someone who wants to add greater location independence, freedom, and flexibility to their lives?

Don't quit your day job yet. Hustle to create a second source of income, and once you are making enough to be able to live solely off the income, feel free to take the leap to full time.

Nora Dunn

 In 2006 Nora sold everything she owned in order to embrace her dreams with no plans of where to go or what to do. She began freelance writing to keep herself fed, and stumbled upon the world of free accommodation. She's started an NGO in Thailand, filmed a TV show in New Zealand, led llama tours, and has housesit for oodles of humans. She now teaches others how to do the same.

You can learn more about Nora at *www. theprofessionalhobo.com.*

What were the first steps you took towards location independence and a more flexible work life?

In 2006, I sold everything I owned to embrace my dreams of long-term travel. I've been on the road ever since, and have since developed a career as a freelance writer and blogger.

How has this helped your life?

My life is entirely different now! I have traveled through or lived in over 50 countries in the last 10 years. I have huge flexibility of where - and when - I work.

How has this helped your business?

I sold my financial planning practice in 2006 before I started to travel, but I've managed to parlay my financial expertise into the niche of the finance of travel. I wrote for travel publications about finance, and I wrote for finance publications about travel! The two topics married on my website, which primarily teaches people how to travel full time in a financially sustainable way.

What have you found the most challenging aspect of travelling or remote working, and how are you combatting it?

Work-life balance on the road is murder. I manage it by traveling slowly, so I have sufficient time to get work done as well as explore. Periods of fast travel need to be intermittent, and most of the time I prefer to stay for at least a month in a place (often longer). In fact, there is a whole contingent of location-independent travelers who have started to burn out (of which I'd say I've recently teetered on the edge of). They're either setting up a home somewhere so they can focus on work, or they're considering selling or changing their location-independent businesses.

Aside from the phone, earphones, laptop, external drive, chargers, clothes, toiletries, credit cards, and passport, what stuff do you always pack that you couldn't do without?

I have my Kindle, a few spiritual chachkies (crystals and whatnot), an ultralight towel, my glow poi (although I'm sadly out of practice), and a headlamp, and I swear by using various packing tools like the Hoboroll.

What other tools, team members, or tasks do you employ to keep your business working well?

I keep things very simple - perhaps too simple. If I want to take my business to another level, I need to start outsourcing more - to both tools and assistants. I have recently started to use virtual assistants for random projects, and it's good.

I use Aweber for newsletters, WP for my site, and OpenOffice for the meat of my writing. Tweetdeck for tweets, YouTube for vlogs (iMovie for editing), Thunderbird for Gmail account management....really not much else!

What advice would you give someone who wants to add greater location independence, freedom, and flexibility to their lives?

I wrote a whole book on the topic: *Working on the Road: The Unconventional Guide to Full-Time Freedom* (*www.workingroad. com*)! To the person who doesn't know where to start or what they can offer to the location-independent mix, I would suggest they identify their skills and passions, and see how they're transferrable to other (money-making) applications.

I would also say that it's a lot of work. But if you're prepared to go the distance, learn the science of online success, and build a satisfying business from the ground up, then it can (literally) open up a world of possibilities.

Jodi Ettenberg

Jodi left her law office in 2008 for what she thought would be a 12-month sabbatical. She developed an addiction for noodle soup, and now her sustenance comes through sharing stories surrounding and behind the foods of the world on *LegalNomads.com*.

What were the first steps you took towards location independence and a more flexible work life?

I quit my job as a lawyer and travelled for two years using my savings first. Then, I decided to see if I could continue building a business flexibly. I did not set out to specifically live as a digital nomad; I fell into it by accident and then pursued it strategically once I realized how rewarding it could be.

How has this helped your life?

Living flexibly has allowed me to build a business around learning as much as possible, experience places around the world, and spend quality time with family. I did not have much family time as a lawyer. As an entrepreneur, being able to move my schedule when needed and ensure that I make the most of enjoying cooking and connecting with my family is a huge benefit.

I've also been able to do self-work and become more of who I want to be because of the time freed up by this work-life arrangement.

How has this helped your business?

As someone who writes about food, flexible work life is an important aspect to why I am able to build this business. When I want to do research, I can embed myself in a city for indefinite periods of time, soaking in the food and history. If I need to hunker down and work, I can do that too. The communities of similar-minded people working without fixed location, or doing what I have done now – mini-expat stints in cities I love – has also meant that business growth is helped by great conversations about strategy and goals.

What have you found the most challenging aspect of travelling or remote working and how are you combatting it?

For me, my health. I'm immunocompromised, and I have struggled over the years with staying healthy as I travel. It has also led to my moving far less than I used to and trying to build up immune health instead of more frequently exposing my immune system to new places.

Aside from the phone, earphones, laptop, external drive, chargers, clothes, toiletries, credit cards, and passport, what stuff do you always pack that you couldn't do without?

Portable chopsticks, sarong, packing cubes (the best), Roost Stand for laptop, portable keyboard and mouse, SparkPlug earplugs, a black blazer, and black boots.

Aside from Google Drive and other main cloud-based services, what is one online application you couldn't do without?

Trello.

What other tools, team members, or tasks do you employ to keep your business working well?

Trello and Canva are integral to work, as well as consistent calls and goal-setting for those I work with.

What advice would you give someone who wants to add greater location independence, freedom and flexibility to their lives?

Figure out what your worst case scenario is, so that you have the backstop of that "what if" figured out. It will allow you to free up the space mentally to focus on actionable steps and skillsets you can work on in order to be flexible. For many people, the decision is hampered by fear of the unknown – completely valid. But if you say, "ok, my worst case is x happens, then I do y," then you are able to set that aside and focus on the task at hand, knowing you've thought through consequences.

Justin Cooke

 Justin went to nuclear power school before finishing off an associates degree from Mesa University, Colorado, USA. From there, he went on to be a loan officer and then a marketing manager, where he learned how to crunch numbers and leverage them in his clients' favor. He is the co-founder of Empire Flippers (*empireflippers.com*), an Inc. 500 company that is the world's top curated marketplace for buying and selling established, profitable online businesses. He also is the co-host of a popular podcast of the same name. Based for a while in Devao in the Philippines, he is currently running his businesses and his podcast while hopping around Southeast Asia and the world.

What were the first steps you took towards location independence and a more flexible work life?

While working as mid-level managers for a SEO company in the US, my business partner and I began scaling an offshore team in the Philippines. As that team grew, we saw an opportunity to turn that team into its own business. We presented our case for "outsourcing ourselves" to the Philippines to run the company to our CEO/CFO, and they went for it.

How has this helped your life?

Being able to work/travel anywhere has given me a much broader view of the world. I'm much happier than I've ever been, and that happiness is reflected in my work as well.

How has this helped your business?

As I'm primarily responsible for our content marketing, traveling around and meeting customers and potential customers has expanded my understanding of where they're at and what they're looking for.

What have you found the most challenging aspect of travelling or remote working and how are you combatting it?

"Fast travel" (staying in one place less than two weeks) can get tiring, especially if you've done it for several months in a row. When it gets a bit too hectic, settling down in one place for two to four months helps balance things out.

Aside from the phone, earphones, laptop, external drive, chargers, clothes, toiletries, credit cards, and passport, what stuff do you always pack that you couldn't do without?

I travel with my podcast microphone (ATR-2100). I'm regularly recording podcast episodes or doing interviews on the road, so that mic plus a pillow fort works in a pinch!

Aside from Google Drive and other main cloud-based services, what is one online application you couldn't do without?

Slack. We use Slack for internal team communication, but also have channels that summarize our Zendesk tickets. I can quickly scroll through each day to see if any problems arise and have easy access to our entire team.

What other tools, team members, or tasks do you employ to keep your business working well?

One of our employees (Mike Swigunski) is our sales-marketing coordinator, but he also has been filling in as our event/travel coordinator. We've been throwing retreats, meetups, and parties, and he's been great at organizing everything for us.

What advice would you give someone who wants to add greater location independence, freedom and flexibility to their lives?

The people that really want to get started often wait for the "right" time, but that time isn't likely to come. I've spoken to so many people that got started with **much** less than you think you need, and they've pulled through just fine. If you really want it, just go for it!

Chris Backe

 Chris began his escape from settled life in 2008 by moving to Seoul, Korea to teach English. He made a commitment to check out one new festival or event each week, eventually leading to sharing his adventures and the book *Offbeat Korea*, containing over 100 of Korea's unusual places. While still in Korea, he met and married a Canadian translator. He's now author to over 20 books and shares his adventures at *OneWeirdGlobe.com*.

What were the first steps you took towards location independence and a more flexible work life?

I guess I asked myself, "What am I doing here?" – take that to mean "What am I accomplishing here?" and "What am I hoping to accomplish here?" I knew that I wanted to travel, so I began looking for ways to make traveling happen. Without realizing it, I had begun when I reached out to apply for a job teaching English in South Korea.

I also began to think about what life would look like if I weren't bound to a specific location. "The world is your oyster," so the parents and professors say when you graduate. But that's a setup to a good question to ask: "If the world were your oyster, what would you do?"

How has this helped your life?

This could require a book of its own... but succinctly... I've had the chance to explore many corners of the globe and find some of the weirdest spots on earth. I met my wife while living abroad, and our lives now are shaped by travel in virtually every conceivable way.

How has this helped your business?

Traveling has fueled my business by giving me things to write about or the chance to see how people around the world have tackled the problems we all have. Thailand has an electric bug zapper that's light years better than your basic old flyswatter. South Korea has some great food, including the distinctive "grill-it-yourself" style of barbecue. It reminds me that creative solutions can be found anywhere and everywhere.

What have you found the most challenging aspect of travelling or remote working, and how are you combatting it?

Finding the time! We normally do "slow travel" – staying in one city for months at a time as a base, venturing out from there to the rest of the country. That doesn't work as well for countries like Canada and North America, so we bought a car and have been "fast traveling" – just a day or two (sometimes three) in each given city. I have so many notes and materials that it's hard to figure out where to start!

Aside from the phone, earphones, laptop, external drive, chargers, clothes, toiletries, credit cards, and passport, what stuff do you always pack that you couldn't do without?

Your basic old-school notebook and pen. I prefer the hardcover notebooks that fit in my camera bag, if only because they'll get taken out and put back in, often while in a hurry! Thicker paper, durable covers... they're worth a few extra bucks to ensure they survive.

Also, duct tape and WD-40. The former to make whatever's moving stops moving, the latter for moving whatever's stopped moving! (In a serious emergency, they have many other purposes as well.)

Aside from Google Drive and other main cloud-based services, what is one online application you couldn't do without?

Not sure about the online part of it, but Picasa and I go way back. It's Google's photo editing tool, and even though it's been discontinued, the software still does most everything I need it to .

What other tools, team members, or tasks do you employ to keep your business working well?

Dropbox, Notes, Google Drive... Honestly, the fewer tools the better.

What advice would you give someone who wants to add greater location independence, freedom, and flexibility to their lives?

Start. Now. Plan if you must, but give yourself a "can't-back-out" date if you're serious. Buy that one-way plane ticket when you spot a bargain, or tell the world you're heading to [insert country here] on [insert date here].

Iva Ursano

 Iva worked 20 years as a hairstylist in Canada before taking the global plunge, which she narrates in her book *The Shear Truth*. Today, "helping others face their fears, chase their dreams and live ridiculously happy lives" is what gets Iva up and going in morning. She also volunteers, helping needy families in Guatemala where she is currently based. You can share in her inspiration at *amazingmemovement. com* or join the over 300,000 who follow her on Facebook.

What were the first steps you took towards location independence and a more flexible work life?

The first step was deciding that was the life I wanted to live and then to figure out how to go about doing it. When you finally get tired of working for someone else under their rule, you get creative right quick.

How has this helped your life?

I'm one million percent happier. I feel incredible freedom, joy, peace, and ridiculous happiness.

How has this helped your business?

It's allowed for me to open up other possible revenue streams by becoming more resourceful. When you work for someone else, often you don't care about helping their business grow, but when it suddenly adds to your income, you come up with all kinds of ideas. Also, you can pick and choose the work you want to do and set your own rate.

What have you found the most challenging aspect of travelling or remote working, and how are you combatting it?

I would have to say the poor Wifi and power outages. Being in Guatemala, sometimes they happen more than I'd like, but fortunately for me, I have great clients that understand when this happens.

Aside from the phone, earphones, laptop, external drive, chargers, clothes, toiletries, credit cards, and passport, what stuff do you always pack that you couldn't do without?

My gemstones.

What other tools, team members, or tasks do you employ to keep your business working well?

I often will pass little jobs off to my son. He's also a solo traveller and is always happy to make some fast cash along the way. This way it frees up some of my time to work on some bigger tasks.

What advice would you give someone who wants to add greater location independence, freedom, and flexibility to their lives?

Don't try to plan too far ahead. Have a goal, figure out how to achieve it, and then let the rest fall into place. Surprising things will show up when you cast your net far and wide. Being a female solo traveller, I need to be slightly street smart/wise and confident. Toss fear out the window because it will stop you from doing lots of cool things. Be open to learning and trying new things. I went from being a hairstylist in a mall in a city in Northern Ontario, Canada, to being a social media manager and freelance writer living in Guatemala. Stay open minded and flexible.

Jimmy Naraine

 Jimmy used to work as an analyst for Goldman Sachs. Today, Jimmy travels the world coaching others to live, define, plan for, and then realize their dreams. His courses on lifestyle design on Udemy have over 50,000 paying customers, and received recognition from Udemy itself.

Read more from Jimmy at *JimmyNaraine.com*.

What were the first steps you took towards location independence and a more flexible work life?

Actually, I started very early. When I was a university student, I would book extremely cheap flights and travel the world during the academic year.

However, I took it to a totally different level during my final year. I had a choice:

1) I could rent a flat or a student dorm ($4,000-6,000/year in the UK) and find a part-time job to cover my expenses. However, I was aware of the fact that it was impossible to get a high level position part time, so I would probably end up working in direct sales or as a waiter. This would mean spending all of my waking hours on working and studying in one city – not a very compelling option.

2) I could hack the system and instead of renting an expensive place, take that money and travel to cheaper locations during the academic year. I would come back to the UK for group projects and exams (and stay on my friend's couch).

Since I like to push my comfort zone, I chose the second option and ended up spending 80% of my time on traveling. Since all the lectures were available online, I didn't miss anything. I spoke to many professors and promised that, even though I may miss certain lectures, I will deliver during exams. I gave them my word.

It was a crazy experiment, but it worked. During my final year I not only travelled to about 15 new countries, but also ended up spending less money than an average student and got a solid degree.

The second experience that I had was while I was working at Goldman Sachs. Even though working hours were very long, I tried to figure out how I could hack the system. I implemented powerful time management strategies and ended up getting more done in less time. I also hacked traveling and ended up going abroad two to three times a month (on the weekends), paying less than many of my colleagues were spending in Mayfair nightclubs.

How has this helped your life?

All of those experiences taught me that you can bend reality to your will. Just because the society imposes certain rules on you doesn't mean that you need to conform to all of them. I realized that, instead of sleepwalking through life, you can design your perfect lifestyle. When you want to cook a delicious meal, you don't just go with the flow and mix up the ingredients randomly. Instead, you carefully shop for what is needed and then follow a proven recipe. The same applies to life. You shouldn't let random circumstances shape your reality. Instead, you can consciously figure out where you want to be, design the right plan of action, and push yourself to implement it day by day.

Location independence is something that I had been craving for a long time, and I feel blessed that it became an inextricable part of my life. My highest value in life is **freedom**, and this is precisely what location independence gives me. It's an amazing sensation to know that you are calling your own shots. It's totally up to you what you're going do and where you're going to be next week, next month, next year. Life is shorter than we think, and having the freedom of mobility allows me to explore this beautiful world. This definitely impacts my overall level of happiness as I connect with amazing individuals across different cultures and appreciate our planet more and more with every single trip.

Also, I can bend the climate to my will. When it's freezing cold in Europe, I spend my time in Southeast Asia or South America. When it's rainy and extremely humid there, I come back to Europe. When I was working for big corporations, I didn't have that flexibility. Now, I may feel like, "I really want to surf," and one week later, I will be actually surfing in Bali, handling my business from a laptop. This is the ultimate freedom.

Finally, I have total freedom of spending as much time as I want with my family and friends. For example, I'm writing those words from Poland, because I casually decided that it would be nice to spend two weeks with my family. This is probably the biggest benefit of running a location-independent business. Many people see their parents/extended family only once or twice a year. When you really think about it, this state of affairs is sad. Life is unpredictable, and seeing your loved ones only once a year is strange in this interconnected world.

How has this helped your business?

Being location independent positively impacts my business as I have a total freedom of embracing opportunities globally. For example, if there is an interesting conference to attend, a potential business partner to meet, or a new opportunity to investigate, you don't need to worry about taking days off. You don't need to worry about your business failing while you are abroad. You simply pack your laptop and go to the airport.

What have you found the most challenging aspect of travelling or remote working and how are you combatting it?

The most challenging part is maintaining a strong work ethic while visiting exotic locations. Naturally, when you are in beautiful places like Thailand, Hawaii, or the Canary Islands, it's easy to forget that you actually have a business to run. Initially, I struggled and had to push myself to get the work done. I was surrounded by holiday goers, and there were temptations everywhere. After all, why would I spend six hours in front of my laptop if I could join a day trip to a nearby island? I had those dilemmas, but I learned that it all comes down to two things:

1) Your social circle

People you spend the most time with have a tremendous impact on the way you think, how you perceive the world, and on your daily actions. When you become a location-independent entrepreneur. it's important that you surround yourself by other people who are in a similar situation. If you spend most of your time with tourists who just want to party and chill on the beach, you are very likely to follow similar patterns. However, when you consciously start building a powerful network and surround yourself with entrepreneurs who actually get work done, you will be more likely to become ultra productive.

2) Your habits

Habits are everything. As humans we often fall into the trap of thinking that all our actions are conscious decisions. However, the reality is that most of the things we do are simply habits we've developed. When you really think about it, most of us we live on autopilot. This is why it's so important to create strong habits that will work for you, not against you.

As long as you develop strong work habits before you leave for your overseas adventure, you will be fine. I recommend performing 80/20 analysis to identify the activities that are crucial for your business success, putting them on a checklist, and making sure that every single day you focus on those critical tasks. Eventually, you develop powerful habits and no longer need the list as a reminder.

I also recommend coming up with a **not** to do list. Every single day it will remind you of the things you should avoid (time-wasting activities – e.g., constantly checking your FB updates).

Aside from the phone, earphones, laptop, external drive, chargers, clothes, toiletries, credit cards, and passport, what stuff do you always pack that you couldn't do without?

1) Even though you wrote "aside from earphones," I need to mention the headphones I simply **can't** travel without, namely Bose QuietComfort. They have such a powerful noise cancellation function that I can't even hear the plane engine during the take off. I travel with them everywhere as they've become an essential tool for increasing my level of focus in a

distracting environment. It no longer matters where I am. Those headphones give me a feeling of peace and help me to get more work done.

2) Whenever I travel I pack healthy snacks: natural protein bars (Quest Nutrition), cashew/Brazilian/other nuts, and OMEGA 3. This approach gives me a lot of flexibility and makes it easier to live a healthy life. When I'm really hungry, I don't need to buy crappy food. I can simply eat a protein bar or some nuts and wait till I find a restaurant that offers something healthy.

3) I always travel with a notepad. Even though I do most of my writing on my laptop, I always like to keep some type of notebook on me. You never know when you will get that fresh idea or a surge of inspiration.

Aside from Google Drive and other main cloud-based services, what is one online application you couldn't do without?

I love using Scrivener for content creation. In my opinion, it's much better than any other solution as it allows you to easily manage your content. You can divide your writing into separate sections/titles. Rearranging the structure is extremely easy, so you can play around with different strategies.

Also, even a major task seems easy when you divide it into smaller steps. It may feel overwhelming to write 20,000 words in a single word document. However, when you split your content into smaller sections in Scrivener, psychologically everything becomes less daunting, and you are less likely to procrastinate.

What other tools, team members, or tasks do you employ to keep your business working well?

I strongly believe in teamwork. Nobody has ever achieved anything remarkable just by themselves. This is why I put a lot of emphasis on working with the right people. For example, I never film videos by myself. Instead, I have a movie crew that is willing to travel with me to remote locations. Thanks to this, I can focus all of my energy on doing the things I'm good at rather than trying to juggle all the balls by myself. I also have a trusted team of advisors so when I have a dilemma or an important decision to make, I can ask for their advice.

Many people say that they can't afford to have a team. Well, I believe that this is just a limiting belief. As my friend Peter Sage always says: "You don't need more money, you simply need a better strategy." If you can't pay people to do certain things for you, simply partner with them. Offer them value other than money. For example, it could be a percentage of the business/ specific project, mentoring them, or providing another service in exchange. There are many examples, but the point is this: Figure out how you can bring value to them other than money and make an agreement that's exciting for both parties. After all, if you work with the right team, you can make 1+1=11.

What advice would you give someone who wants to add greater location independence, freedom, and flexibility to their lives?

First of all, figure out what your vision is. The worst thing that can happen to you is not failing at accomplishing your goals. The worst thing that can happen to you is accomplishing the wrong goals. You get to the finish line just to realize that this is not what you really wanted. This is why it's so important to firstly define your true vision, a snapshot of your ideal life.

Based on that, you figure out your long- and short-term goals. While you are working on them, keep asking yourself: "What can I do so those goals help me to become more location independent?"

One common limiting belief people have is that being location independent and living abroad must be extremely expensive. However, this couldn't be further from the truth. Of course, if you fly first class and stay in fancy hotels, you will end up burning a lot of money. However, if you do it in a smart way and live like a local person, you will most probably end up spending less money than at home (especially when you are traveling to places like Southeast Asia, South America, or Southern/Eastern Europe).

The problem is that most people can't understand it till they take that leap. This is why I recommend "test driving" location independence. Instead of making the big decision that you will be a full-time traveler, go overseas for several weeks and see how you feel. In most cases, organizing a trip like this will be eye opening, and once you experience the freedom, you will never go back to your regular life.

Learn not to do everything and start outsourcing tasks that:

a) you don't like doing.

b) are very simple/repetitive.

c) are too complicated for you and an expert could complete them 3-10x faster.

You can find plenty of potential virtual assistants on Upwork. I know that hiring someone for the first time can be scary. This is why I encourage you to start small. Hire somebody just for a few hours and play around, see how you feel. Very soon you will realize that outsourcing can save you a ton of time and energy. You can then use some of that free time to focus on critical tasks that will bring you the most value.

Shayna Oliveira

 Shanya is a 30-something Connective native. A vacation romance spurred Shanya to take the first step towards location independence by asking her job to let her work remotely in Brazil. They agreed, then she asked to work only ¼ of the time. They agreed again. Now she runs an English education website with over 80,000 students. When she's not working on her business, she does Capoeira (Brazilian martial art dance), and she's happily married her to her original muse.

You can find out more about Shayna at *www.espressoenglish. net*.

What were the first steps you took towards location independence and a more flexible work life?

I had been working full-time in New York City for about three years when I asked to work remotely from Brazil - the company agreed. Later, I wanted to reduce my hours from full-time to quarter-time - they agreed again. This freed up plenty of time for me to start my own business on the side teaching English online. Over the next few years I grew that side business to a large and profitable, one, which is now my full-time focus. I can run it from anywhere with an Internet connection.

How has this helped your life?

I'm so much happier with the freedom I now have. I can choose exactly where I want to live, as well as when and how much to work. I can travel and take time off without having to ask for permission. It's been an amazing experience, and I hope to live the rest of my life with this flexibility.

How has this helped your business?

Being location independent and having control of my schedule allow me to travel to meetups and conferences with other entrepreneurs. These meetups have been incredibly valuable both for inspiration and for exchanging real, impactful business advice that takes my business to the next level.

What have you found the most challenging aspect of travelling or remote working and how are you combatting it?

I tend to turn into a beast when something goes wrong on my business website. At one point, my hosting provider was doing a planned server migration on a Saturday while I was traveling. When I checked in later, I discovered they had migrated the wrong website, everything was down, and I couldn't get it back online. I spent several hours sweating bullets while dealing with tech support. After a stressful day, everything worked out, and my site got back online.

Aside from the phone, earphones, laptop, external drive, chargers, clothes, toiletries, credit cards, and passport, what stuff do you always pack that you couldn't do without?

My capoeira clothes. I do capoeira (an Afro-Brazilian martial art and dance), and there are groups all over the world. So wherever I go, I visit the local group to train and make friends.

Aside from Google Drive and other main cloud-based services, what is one online application you couldn't do without?

FollowUpThen - I use it to send emails out of my inbox, and they will return at a time I specify. It's great for keeping my inbox clear while still being sure to remind me of things exactly when needed.

What other tools, team members, or tasks do you employ to keep your business working well?

I'm a minimalist when it comes to both tools and team - I work alone and use few tools! But I've found some good subcontractors on PeoplePerHour.com, and the tool that runs the backend of my online course business is MemberMouse.

What advice would you give someone who wants to add greater location independence, freedom and flexibility to their lives?

Don't ask "Can I do this?" which is a yes or no question. Instead, ask yourself "**How** can I do this?" and then come up with creative ways to accomplish your goal. There are many paths to freedom and flexibility, and I believe everyone can design a lifestyle that they enjoy, if they proactively pursue it.

James Allen

 American James Allen was living and teaching English in Japan in 2003, when his wife became pregnant with their only daughter. By the time his daughter was born in early 2004, he was making a full-time living selling and exporting underground comic books and was able to quit his teaching position just in time for her birth. The family has been location independent and traveling since 2011, living in and traveling to over ten different countries and homeschooling their daughter along the way.

Read more about James at *javanomad.com*.

What were the first steps you took towards location independence and a more flexible work life?

I have been making a full-time living online since late 2003 and have been location independent since early 2005. I was living and teaching English in Japan in 2003 knowing full well I had no interest in being stuck in a university classroom in Tokyo for the rest of my life - especially since I had a child on the way and wanted to be able to be around while she was growing up. So I began looking for things in Japan I could sell online for a profit. I did all my research and testing between and after classes and on the weekend. Eventually I stumbled across a product that was in high demand outside Japan, was cheap to source in Japan, and could be sold at a massive mark-up on eBay. By the time my daughter was born in early 2004, I was making a full-time living selling and exporting underground comic books and was able to quit my teaching position just in time for her birth. The online marketing skills I began learning from this business - which was **not** location independent - translated over the following year into online income streams that did not require physical products. At that point I became location independent as well.

How has this helped your life?

For the past 12 years, I have been able to live and travel around the world with my wife and daughter, growing and learning together as a family. Following our interests and passions as we see fit. I can't imagine any other way of living.

How has this helped your business?

My various income streams (I wouldn't call them "businesses") are secondary to our lifestyle. I spend just enough time "working" to cover our upcoming expenses for experiencing. While we were still running our comic book business, I spent a year straight learning and honing my copywriting skills. Once I could "write words that sell," I knew I would not have to worry about income ever again. Copywriting skills translate to so many areas of online marketing - even as the technology has rapidly and dramatically changed - that I am always able to find new, interesting, and successful ways to generate income online.

What have you found the most challenging aspect of travelling or remote working and how are you combatting it?

I left my home country 15 years ago. I've only been back to visit twice. I left my adopted home of Japan nearly six years ago. We've been travelling ever since. There does come a point where you start thinking you want a "home base" again. Part of the journey then starts becoming finding a **home** again.

Aside from the phone, earphones, laptop, external drive, chargers, clothes, toiletries, credit cards, and passport, what stuff do you always pack that you couldn't do without?

My passion over the past several years has been learning about the coffee industry - with a focus on specialty bean production and roasting. Because of this, I actually lug around an extra suitcase filled with coffee equipment - including a very heavy sample roaster.

Aside from Google Drive and other main cloud-based services, what is one online application you couldn't do without?

My Aweber autoresponder account.

What other tools, team members, or tasks do you employ to keep your business working well?

My overhead and toolkit mainly consists of my web hosting account, my autoresponder account, and my Amazon S3 account. Notebook. Pen.

What advice would you give someone who wants to add greater location independence, freedom, and flexibility to their lives?

Learn to write copy that converts. Once you can do that, the world is yours.

Princess Villareal

 Princess Villareal was born in the Philippines and was a ghostwriter for Bart Baggett, owner of Handwriting University based in Los Angeles.

After completing her degree in marketing management in 2015, she traveled to the US to help her father with his business but soon starting selling cosmetics and fashion items online through Amazon and eBay, as well as through her own site.

She returned to the Philippines via a few other places, including Chiang Mai, Thailand, and is now considering her next moves in business

More about Princess can be found at *thecesiacollection.com*.

What were the first steps you took towards location independence and a more flexible work life?

The first step was making the decision of what lifestyle I want and am comfortable with. Traveling is fun but not for everybody. I find it really useful when I'm in the middle of my emotional journey of a certain stage in life. Researching is very, very essential, whether it is for the business that you are putting up or which country is your next destination. Testing is fun too, so be fearless.

How has this helped your life?

It developed my capacity to kinda "Sing in the middle of the storm." There's a lot to think about when you're working remotely.

How has this helped your business?

I would say that it's improved my mental stamina and emotional intelligence. It helped my business go in different angles. That's not something you can just find online, but you learn things the hard way.

What have you found the most challenging aspect of travelling or remote working, and how are you combatting it?

Being a woman is very challenging. Men can just bring a light backpack, and that's it. We women bring a lot of things with us. I brought about 50-60 kg of luggage from the Philippines to Vegas, to Chiang Mai, and to the Philippines again. It wasn't fun, because normally I have to take about three to four connecting flights, and the extra luggage fees are expensive.

Aside from the phone, earphones, laptop, external drive, chargers, clothes, toiletries, credit cards, and passport, what stuff do you always pack that you couldn't do without?

My SLR Camera, my make-up, my books, notebooks, blow dryer, and lastly, my shoes.

Aside from Google Drive and other main cloud-based services, what is one online application you couldn't do without?

Asana (which was introduced by my New Yorker friend) and the communication apps.

What advice would you give someone who wants to add greater location independence, freedom, and flexibility to their lives?

I started as a very curious person and discovered that there are things that people are really good at faking. Be true to yourself but have faith as well. Starting up a business and being location independent are not just walks in the park. Do a lot of research, and don't be scared to start something everyday to keep you moving. Have a goal as well, and please don't fall into drinking almost every night. For sure there are so many productive things you can do and discover along the way. Be strong.

Jacob Hiller

Jacob Hiller created the Jump Manual (*JumpManaul.com*) ten years ago and has since sold over $6 million worth of e-books and and white-label software. Soon after getting married, his wife got a job in Germany, so they left the US. They still haven't returned and have lived in over 45 countries, and four years ago, they were joined by their son.

What were the first steps you took towards location independence and a more flexible work life?

The first thing I did was have a business model that allowed me to work anywhere – so I can work as long as there is internet. I got married, and nine years ago she got a job in Germany. We were basically travelling within the first year, and my business started to grow. Later on things got very flexible when I got my team involved – even more so when I got my team doing everything I do – answering my emails, doing all the important stuff. And we have an emergency system set up. Then I could go on cruises and be away for weeks or even more. I had freedom basically to do whatever I wanted, and the business could run itself even if I wasn't working on it.

How has this helped your life?

It's fun to be engaged in your work, but it's also fun to unplug and to explore. For me, traveling has enabled me to understand, not so much the country but myself more. Because each country tells me a little bit more about the expectations and the cultural norms that I grew up with. And I feel like every country to be another piece of where I'm juxtaposed in the global world culture. It gives me peace of mind and a certain sense of freedom, which is amazing.

How has this helped your business?

Sometimes it doesn't help because when you work anywhere, anytime, sometimes you just don't do it. That's why I like to have a team because I organize the team in such a way where I could just talk to them on my phone and give them tasks. And they update me on my phone, so it's very easy to have an idea and make it come to fruition just by speaking.

What have you found the most challenging aspect of travelling or remote working and how are you combatting it?

At first, it was finding good Internet. Sometimes it's finding places to shoot videos. I'd like to have decent lighting for my videos. So Internet was an issue. With the team, things become easier because, while I don't have good internet, I'm not uploading the videos and doing all these things, because that's what they are doing. So that was the biggest issue.

Aside from the phone, earphones, laptop, external drive, chargers, clothes, toiletries, credit cards, and passport, what stuff do you always pack that you couldn't do without?

I have my own bag packing system, and that makes moving from one place to another very easy. I have bags tied together with a hanger on top. I have six of them. So when moving to a place, I just have to hang them up and have them slide down.

I don't think there's much I can do without. And these days, I even don't use a laptop. I just use my iPad Pro, which is even better because I have don't have to carry a big charger or a big laptop, which makes things very portable. I like having a very nice back pack and very nice messenger bag. It just makes me feel nice and portable. Sometimes like having a mini skateboard.

Regarding equipment I have a gorilla tripod for my iPhone. A good phone is important for my work of course, so I'll always get the latest and greatest phone.

Aside from Google Drive and other main cloud-based services, what is one online application you couldn't do without?

For me it's all about communication nowadays rather than getting stuff done. I don't get stuff done. My team gets stuff done. So communication, task management, and project management are most important for me. So I use Asana – I love Asana – and I use a very specific style with Asana. I love Whatsapp as well. Those were the two big ones for communication for me.

What other tools, team members, or tasks do you employ to keep your business working well?

When I got into ads, I brought in a full-time partner in America, and we did a profit share. He's very good. He handles a lot of the paid advertising we do. I have a lot of affiliates. I love my affiliates because they give me leverage. And about five other team members in the Philippines, and I go visit them once a year. We're very tight, and we communicate regularly. Also, I do white label software as well (people put their logo on my software and then market it), and I like that a lot too because it gives me the freedom to just make sure that everything is working, and they do the marketing because the marketing can be a lot of work.

What advice would you give someone who wants to add greater location independence, freedom, and flexibility to their lives?

Well, definitely, find a business model that doesn't require you to be at point A or point B obviously. I would say the team is really big. Find a team, take the time to find out what tasks you don't need to do, find the things that you're absolutely needed for. Try to outsource. That's been the really big thing for me.

Final Thoughts and Thanks

I had been meaning to write this book for a while.

When I'd asked friends and associates online and off what they'd like me to do next, they'd often mention my location independence as something they were interested in. This baffled me at first.

Why would you want *me* to talk about *that*? There are people who've been on the road for much longer than I. Also, this life isn't for everyone. Most people want to stay home.

But the more I thought about it, the more I realized that this subject could help everyone. Everyone could use a bit of freedom and flexibility in their lives. I could help some people, I thought.

But I didn't want to write "becoming a digital nomad" or "a guidebook for location independence," and after going through titles like "flexible living" or "freedom of location," I stuck on the rather grandiose "new freedom."

Please, don't ask me why.

Like everything I do, the idea comes first, the marketing plan second. Which is why I quite obviously suck at marketing.

But I'm good with that. Online marketers often preach: "Put three benefits into the title" or "Define your avatar" or "Niche down to a specific definable purpose." And I think that's why so much online marketing literature is bland, formulaic, and borderline scammy.

At least that's what I like to tell myself.

The other reason I wrote this book was, quite frankly, because I wanted to. I'd been down about my first foray into e-commerce with Fulfilment by Amazon as well as a drop in my passive income for the first time in a couple of years, and I wanted to do something enjoyable.

And it was. At first.

The final read throughs, as well as the pain of deciding on the title and the cover, have reminded me why I haven't written a book for a year or so. It's been a great gestation period, but the birthing pains are extremely unpleasant.

I apologize for the book's obvious flaws.

What's so new about the new freedom that wasn't new about *The 4-Hour Workweek*? Well, a lot has happened in the last nine years. Yes, it's been nearly ten years. And, this is the new freedom according to Rob. We couldn't do this five years ago, and the world has been here for 6 billion. So that's "new"!

This book is far from perfect. It includes a lot of my personal experience. I like to write from experience. I apologize from the over-emphasis on Thailand, the repetitions, the lack of money-making strategies, etc. There are some sections I could have written more on, no doubt.

But, sometimes you've got to let your baby go out into the world and hope for the best.

Thank yous

I'd like to thank anyone who's ever known me, my family, my mum, and my dad, who died last year. (I had a dream about him last night and I told him I loved him. I'm really happy about that.)

I'd like to thank Tim Ferriss, Matt Mullenweg, Glen Allsopp, and Cody McKibben for their inspiration.

I'd mostly like to thank Andrew Lentz for his ongoing help with suggestions, edits, idea for the book subtitle, and extra content, particularly on the cities I didn't know about.

More thanks:

- Elizabeth Stockton of Clear Sharp Writing for editing and proofreading.
- Jyotsna Ramachandran at Happy Self Publishing for the red balloon cover.
- Azim Uddin for the print typography.
- Hynek Palatin for the digital version (and for his great company when I was in Prague).
- The fifty plus members of my "street team" who read the first draft.
- So many people (too many to mention) who made various suggestions for titles, covers, ideas.

I love you all. So very much.

Don't forget to pop by my website and say "hi": *RobCubbon.com*.

Remember, I have six free video courses on my site. The courses are about creating websites, WordPress, email marketing, and a course about how to earn passive income. This is some of my best content, and it is especially aimed at people who want to work for themselves, earn more money online, and live the new freedom.

You can get these free courses here: *robcubbon.com/freecourses*

If you've enjoyed this book, I would so appreciate it if you could either recommend it to a friend or **review it on Amazon**.

You may also enjoy one of my other books. Here is my Amazon author page: *www.amazon.com/Rob-Cubbon/e/ B00G5VEY14*

Rob Cubbon

Chiang Mai, November 2016.

Copyright and Disclaimers

Legal Disclaimer:

This report is not intended to be a source of legal, business, accounting, or financial advice. It is based on the personal experiences and observations of the author. Readers are encouraged to seek out the services of competent professionals for such advice.

The author and publisher have made every effort to supply accurate and thorough information in the creation of this report. But, they offer no warranty and accept no responsibility for any loss or damages of any kind that may be incurred by the reader as a result of actions arising from the use of information found in this report.

The author and publisher reserve the right to make any changes they deem necessary to future versions of the publication to ensure its accuracy.

The reader assumes all responsibility for the use of the information within this report.

If you do not accept the terms of this agreement, please return the product immediately for a full refund, at which point you must destroy any copies of the publication in your possession.